CENACLE LIBRARY
2269 Wauwatosa Avenue
WAUWATOSA 13, WIS.

========

Life membership one dollar.

Fee of ten cents on each book.

Books may be kept one month only.

All books kept over the month are subject to a fine of two cents a day.

Fees and over due charges are strictly collected.

Out of courtesy to our members notification will be sent when a book is one week over due.

Lost or damaged books must be replaced.

THE SERVILE STATE

The Servile State

by HILAIRE BELLOC

"... If we do not restore the Institution
of Property we cannot escape restoring
the Institution of Slavery; there is no
third course."

FIRST AMERICAN EDITION

With an Introduction by

CHRISTIAN GAUSS

New York

HENRY HOLT AND COMPANY

To

E. S. P. Haynes

CONTENTS

CONTENTS

INTRODUCTION TO THE FIRST AMERICAN EDITION

WHEN *THE SERVILE STATE* FIRST AP-peared in England in 1912, a considerable part of its importance lay in the fact that it contained much in the way of prophecy. That books have their fates, as the Latin proverb holds, is admirably illustrated in its history. Most dictionaries still tell us that thirty years is the life span of a generation. Many of Mr. Belloc's works have received as cordial a reception in this country as abroad and American editions were available here simultaneously with their publication abroad. In this brief treatise or longish tract, Belloc presented the essence of his thinking on political, social and economic problems. It was, as we shall see, to have a direct bearing upon the thinking of a sig-nificant group of American thinkers and reformers. Yet it was to have to wait more than a generation before being made more generally available in this first American edition. It is interesting to speculate upon the reasons for this long delay and a brief sum-mary may throw some light on the character of Belloc's volume.

In 1912 *The Servile State* offered no threat to our complacency; neither was any large wing of the Amer-ican public interested in Belloc's indictment of that "evil thing capitalism." It was generally assumed that capitalism was the basis of a self-regulating "sys-tem of free enterprise." Most American reformers advocated socializing "the means of production," which meant having the government take them over, and it was assumed that this process could be carried on with impunity and would have only beneficent results for the working class. Belloc was so clearly in opposition to both these wings of American public opinion, that his major thesis could hardly have received a sympathetic hearing. But there was another consideration which made the problem to which he was directing attention seem remote. Belloc was deeply concerned about a type of legislation which was being introduced in Prussia and in England, avowedly designed to improve the condition of the "proletariat." Most Americans then refused to admit that we had any proletariat. In tracing capitalism back in its English setting, he found it rooted in the landless condition of a very large part of the English population, before the Industrial Revolution began. Most Americans then, only a quarter of a century removed from the open frontier and the era of free lands, would have dismissed the problem with an "It can't happen here."

If *The Servile State* could have been dismissed with a shrug in 1912, the reasons why it cannot be so dismissed now will be evident in the course of even a brief introduction. I make no plea for full acceptance either of Belloc's historical analysis or of his theories, and admit that there are many passages which may

INTRODUCTION

still annoy American readers today. One of them is his unorthodox analysis of capitalism, which we have mentioned. It is generally held that modern capitalism took its present form as the result of the industrial revolution and the methods of production then introduced, and that in this process, a new class, the bourgeoisie, acquired political power and supplanted the older feudal, landed aristocracy. Belloc holds that by 1700 England had already become capitalist in that she was already "cursed with a very large proletarian class," and since the industrial system arose in and spread from England, it proceeded upon this capitalist model. Only the already rich land owners could furnish the wealth required, and the rise of the bourgeoisie as a new class receives no attention in Belloc's analysis.

Many Americans will admit that much of the capital required in the early development of American railroads and factories was provided by English capitalists, but they may well refuse to accept the conclusion that the course of the industrial revolution in our country was determined by this pattern. They will hold that the mill hand of 1830 in Lowell, Massachusetts, was not hopelessly landless like his counterpart in England. A consideration of one aspect of the situation in America should, however, give us pause. Arthur Schlesinger, Sr., has said that the most important single fact about the discovery of America was that it changed the ratio of man to land. In virtually all of the European countries from which our colonists and immigrants came, all available lands had already been preempted. Here, the lands still waiting for their first occupants seemed limitless. There can be little doubt that the immigrant who came as an indentured servant to Virginia for a three or five year term came not only with the intention of increasing his income, but of improving his social status as well. Our legal terminology still indicates this. When he became the owner of land he would possess "real estate," and be his own "landlord." This consciousness of possessing status may well have been one of the factors that made our frontier settlements the freest communities our modern world has known. That sense of landlord status has now certainly been lost by many Americans. In this respect, Jefferson's fear that the development of factories and growth of cities must threaten our liberties, was justified. On this count, Belloc is a Jeffersonian. He holds that the wage-earner is losing his status as a free contracting agent and is being reduced to a quite inferior status as a ward of the state. The stakes which the wage-earner is playing for when he demands security from the capitalist by state action on measures like the minimum wage, unemployment insurance, are too high. Even if he wins, he is, according to Belloc, by way of losing his freedom. In the ancient forms of the Servile State, security and

INTRODUCTION

subsistence were the reward guaranteed to the slave by his servile status. If in our statutes, instead of employer we substituted the word master, and instead of employee, the word serf or slave, the drift of our times would be clearer. To save capitalism you must get rid of "restrictive ownership or of freedom, or of both."

It is worth reminding ourselves that in his *Ancient Law*, Sir Henry Maine offered it as his conclusion that "the movement of the progressive societies has hitherto been a movement from status to contract." To reverse that process and to pass from freedom of contract to acceptance of status is, for Belloc, no satisfactory solution for the ever increasing instability of the capitalistic structure. Belloc also rejects as a solution the collectivist theory which "the capitalist state tends to breed," since in action it produces something utterly different from collectivism and gives us again the servile state.

Historians will object to the virtually exclusive rôle which Belloc assigns to the Church in the gradual elimination of slavery from the ancient forms of the servile state. His attitude is the more remarkable since it is Catholic scholars in general who have given fullest credit to the important rôle which the Stoics played in developing the concept of natural law with its corollary of inalienable human rights so familiar to us all in the Declaration of Independence. In other

xiii

respects, Belloc is justified in making claims for the particular service rendered by the Church of Rome. Its long prohibition of the taking of interest (usury) and its doctrine of the just price checked, though they could not prevent, the development of capitalism. Scholars like Max Weber and R. H. Tawney have made it plain that most Protestant churches were clearly more willing to allow the devil to take the hindmost. God helps those who help themselves, came to be the motto particularly acceptable to our puritan ancestors. Helping oneself was interpreted by them primarily as helping oneself to get ahead on the economic level, and when this came to be regarded as a possible outer and visible sign of divine grace, the rush for profit received a quasi-religious sanction.

From what hills then may we expect our hope to come? Belloc holds that the servile state is not even historically the only form of political and social organization. Between the ancient and modern capitalistic forms of the servile state there was, in the late middle ages, an interregnum, a form which he calls the Distributive State. In this state there were more varied and better balanced forms of ownership. On estates and in villages there were common lands and privately owned lands. Guilds held in common only the property necessary to their cooperative life. The individual member owned the instruments of his trade save where they were so expensive as to necessitate

corporate control. Self-governing corporations regulated production so that the misery and insecurity of
the proletariat was unknown. We may find Belloc's
historical sketch over-idealized. What is important to
his thesis is that there has been a form of social organization which tended to distribute property more
widely instead of concentrating it in ever fewer hands,
and that if we are to escape "the moral anarchy of
capitalism" social institutions with a similar distributive tendency must again be created.

It is difficult to assign absolute priority for the
invention of phrases which have provoked fruitful
discussion, but Belloc seems to have been the first
to use this phrase, the Distributive State, and it is
certain that this treatise did much to stimulate that
group of American thinkers we have mentioned, who
advocate economic decentralization and who sometimes call themselves "distributists."

We have said that when *The Servile State* was first
published it would not greatly have interested any
large body of American readers. A prophecy of what
would happen in Germany and England, where the
greatest fear of the mass of men was not the fear of
the punishments which the laws could impose, but
the fear of losing their jobs, was not then our affair.
Too much of that prophecy has been fulfilled and the
problem has become America's problem as well. We
too realize now that if the inventiveness of men along

scientific and technical lines is not to become a destructive force in human affairs, it is clearly necessary that we devote far more constructive thinking to the purposes and forms of social organization. Belloc has tried to do this by dealing with the gap between what one of our distinguished American theologians has called "moral man and immoral society." His book now bristles with challenges to our earlier complacency. If it is true, as a philosopher has said, that there is no problem which the human reason can propound which the human reason cannot reason out, he has rendered a fruitful service. Whether we agree with him or not, he has made a new and sharper statement of our problem. Catch penny and catch vote remedies are not here proposed, but those who are interested in reconstituting a free society cannot fail, in the light of two World Wars, to find here much to their purpose.

CHRISTIAN GAUSS.

PREFACE TO THE NEW EDITION

THIS BOOK WAS FIRST PUBLISHED IN THE year before the War. That catastrophe had not come upon us, when a second edition was called for. The abnormal years that followed were ill suited to general economic thought: they were too actively concerned with immediate economic troubles. But I am told that a third edition is now demanded, and I am glad it should be so; for I am convinced that the subject with which it deals is the chief political matter of our time.

I have changed nothing in the text, not even terms of currency dating from before the War; for a general argument of this kind and the general tendency with which it is concerned are little affected by matters of passing interest. I have not even modified the sentence in which I say that State Collectivism can show no working example, for the Russian Revolution, which took place four years after my first edition appeared, has *not* produced a Collectivist State; on the contrary it has produced a State the vast bulk of which—some nine-tenths—have, by it, been confirmed as peasant-owners.

Neither has it seemed worth while to emphasise the points on which advance towards the Servile State has been made since the first publication: they are obvious to all: the rapid growth of monopoly on the one hand and the new measures for providing Proletarian security and sufficiency on the other. To which might be added the increasing demand for some official machinery for making combined action on the part of the Proletariat impossible.

I had, indeed, thought it advisable at one moment to add some words on the term "property" in order to point out that a wide distribution of property *in insignificant amounts* was no weakening but rather a bolstering up of Capitalism. All own something. Even a tramp owns, I suppose, his broken boots. The essential of Capitalism is a refusal to the many of Property *in significant amounts* and the decline of small estates. I had, I say, thought at one moment of making this clearer by a few pages of expanded statement. But I decided, after some hesitation, to leave the argument as it was. For I considered that those to whom the argument for existing small property appeals—those whom our Capitalist press bemuses with the mere numbers of holders in Railway stock or the National Debt—were hardly of the kind who would follow a serious economic discussion.

HILAIRE BELLOC.

January 1st, 1927.

PREFACE TO SECOND EDITION

WITH THE ISSUE OF A SECOND EDITION of this book the author may perhaps be excused for adding, by way of Preface, a few words upon the thesis it maintains and the method through which that thesis is treated.

It appears the more necessary to do so because a careful comparison of the reviews and other expressions of opinion which it has received convinces the author that parts of his argument are liable to misconception. It would be a pity to correct such misconception by any changes in a completed book; a few words set down here by way of Preface should be sufficient for the purpose.

First: I would point out that the argument contained in the book bears no relation to the common accusation levelled against Socialists (that is, Collectivists) that life in a Socialist State would be so subject to regulation and order as to be unduly oppressive. With this common objection to the reform advocated by Socialists I have nothing to do in this book, nor can it touch my subject at any point. This book does not discuss the Socialist State. Indeed it is the very heart of my thesis that we are not, as a fact, approaching Socialism at all, but a very different state of society; to wit, a society in which the Capitalist class shall be even more powerful and far more secure than it is at present: a society in which the proletarian mass shall not suffer from particular regulations, oppressive or beneficent, but shall change their status, lose their present legal freedom, and be subject to compulsory labour.

Next, I would beg my readers to believe that I have not attempted to set up this thesis as a warning or as a piece of gloom. I say nowhere in the book that the re-etsablishment of slavery would be a bad thing as compared with our present insecurity, and no one has a right to read such an opinion into this book. Upon the contrary, I say clearly enough that I think the tendency towards the re-establishment of slavery is due to the very fact that the new conditions may be found more tolerable than those obtaining under Capitalism. Which state of society might reasonably be preferred—the re-establishment of slavery or the maintenance of Capitalism—would make an ample subject for another book: but that alternative does not concern this volume or the thesis therein maintained.

Finally, I would beg such of my readers as are Socialist by conviction not to misconceive my opinion upon what their movement is effecting. The most sincere and the best writer among the English Socialists wrote of this book that the author had mistaken the "Social Reform" of the professional politicians for Socialism, and that while this "Social Reform" might be tending towards the re-establishment of compulsory labour for the benefit of an owning class, yet Socialism had no such intention or tendency.

Now, I never made such an error. What I have said in this book is that the object of the Socialist (a very simple and clear matter—the putting of the means of production into the hands of politicians to hold in trust for the community) is not in practice being approached; that we are not, *as a matter of fact,* coming nearer towards the collective ownership of the means of production, but that we *are* rapidly coming nearer to the establishment of compulsory labour among an unfree majority of non-owners for the benefit of a free minority of owners. And I say that this tendency is due to the fact that the Socialist ideal, in conflict with and yet informing the body of Capitalism, produces a third thing very different from the Socialist ideal—to wit, the Servile State. It is important to have this point clear, and perhaps a metaphor is needed. I will present one.

A traveller sincerely desirous of escaping from the cold climate of the mountains conceives the obvious plan of going South, where he will find lower and warmer land. With this project in his head he finds a river flowing in a southerly direction and he says, "If I travel upon this River I will reach my object the more readily." One who has studied the nature of that mountainous region may say to him: "You are in error. The very evils from which you are trying to escape, the mountains, are so constructed that in a

short while you will find them diverting the course
of this River northward again. Indeed, if you will
look at your compass you will see that the big bend
has already begun."

The traveller is the Socialist. The South which he
desires to reach is the Collectivist State. The River is
modern "Organised Reform." The Northern country
where the mountain River will ultimately find a quiet
bed is a society reposing upon compulsory labour.

A man thus speaking to the traveller would not be
denying either the sincerity of his desire to get south-
ward or his belief that the River would lead him
there; all he would be denying would be the fact that
the River does lead him there.

There is only one discrepancy in this parallel, which
is that the traveller in the metaphor could, upon being convinced of his error, leave the River and get
South by land. That would correspond in the case of
the Socialist to a bold policy of Confiscation, to a
taking of the means of production from the hands of
those who now own them and to a placing of them
in the hands of politicians to be held in trust for the
community.

I nowhere deny in my book that this is ideally possible: just as it is ideally possible that to-morrow all
Englishmen shall take and preserve for twenty-four
hours a vow of silence. What I say is that nothing
like it or approaching it has ever been done or is now

being done. I say further, what is of capital importance, that with every step taken along the existing lines of change in our industrial society we are making it more and more difficult to retrace such steps, to abandon the accepted method and to pursue the Collectivist ideal. The path of Confiscation, the only way by which Socialists can reach their goal, gets more and more remote with every new and positive economic reform, undertaken, remember, with the aid and under the advice of Socialists themselves.

These, then, are the three main points, I think, upon which there has been misconception and against which I hope I may warn the reader. To recapitulate:—

(1) The misconception that I have used the word "servile" in some rhetorical sense of "irksome" or "oppressive," whereas I have attempted to use it only under the limits of my definition, viz., That labour is "servile" which is undertaken not in fulfilment of contract but under the compulsion of positive law and which attaches to the status of the labourer, and is performed for the benefit of others who are under no such compulsion.

(2) The misconception that the advent of the Servile State is put forward for a warning or a danger-sign: I am concerned in this book to say how and why we *are* approaching it; not whether we *should* approach it.

(3) The misconception that I have mis-stated the

aims and the convictions of Socialists. These aims and convictions are simple enough, and my point is not that they are either illusions or doubtful, but that in point of fact we are not heading towards them and that the effect of Socialist doctrine upon Capitalist society is to produce a third thing different from either of its two begetters—to wit, the Servile State.

Apart from these three main points I must, in view of certain less intelligent criticisms the book has provoked, mention one or two other matters.

Thus, my argument that slavery was slowly transformed and that the old Pagan Servile State slowly approached a Distributive State under the influence of the Catholic Church is not a piece of special pleading put forward to please my co-religionists. It is a plain piece of historical fact which anyone can verify for himself, and which many do not regard as an advantage, but as a disadvantage inflicted upon humanity by the advent of this religion. Whether the servile institution be a good or a bad thing, it did, as a matter of fact, slowly disappear as Catholic civilisation developed; and it has, as a matter of fact, slowly begun to return where Catholic civilisation has receded.

Nor have I said that the goal of a completely free Distributive State was ever reached. I have said that it was in process of formation when the disruption of our united European civilisation in the sixteenth century arrested its development and slowly produced, in this country especially, Capitalism in its stead.

Again, examples of State regulation and of State or Municipal economic enterprise increasing rapidly among us obviously do not affect my argument. Unless or until these are based upon a policy of Confiscation they are no more an example of Socialism than the explosion of gunpowder is an example of warfare. They are no more "Socialistic efforts" or "beginnings" or "experiments in Socialism" than fireworks at the Crystal Palace are "military" efforts or "beginnings" or "experiments in militarism." Socialism would indeed involve such regulations and such municipal enterprise just as war involves the explosion of gunpowder; but they do not form its essence at all. Its essence consists in vesting in trust with the politicians what is now private property. When Municipal and State enterprise accompanied by Municipal and State regulation is based upon loans instead of Confiscation, nay, loans devised to *avoid* Confiscation, it is a negation of Socialism; and I have shown that attempts to mask the capitalist character of such operations by the machinery of sinking funds and the rest are logically worthless. You cannot "buy out" Capitalism.

I need not point out what steps have been taken, even in the very short time since this book first appeared, in the direction which it is intended to explain.

We already have Wages Boards in one great industry; we shall shortly have them in more. We already have the registration of the proletariat with name, address, movement from place to place, nature of illness when illness is incurred, supposed or real "malingering," indulgence in this or that vice (such as drink), domestic habits, nature of employment, and all the rest of it very nearly complete, and *imposed by the wealthier classes who are the actual gatherers of the Poll Tax upon which this registration is based.* We have through the Labour Exchanges a system which will soon be equally complete and by which every member of the proletariat will ultimately be similarly registered as a worker, his tendencies to rebellion against Capital known and their frequency set down, how far he is willing to serve Capitalism, whether and when he has refused service, and if so where and why.

The reader will be interested to note amid the accidents and reactions of the years immediately before us the slow perfection of this system: registration and control of the proletariat, with its necessary and fatal approach towards the term of compulsory labour. But I think in justice to my book I should point out to that same reader the meaning of its concluding pages. No change in European society arrives at completion unless it is universal throughout Europe. Capitalism is not thus universal; it is developed in

PREFACE TO SECOND EDITION

very different degrees in different parts of Europe; the advent of servitude is therefore a probability differing in degree with different portions of European society. It is evident that the example of economic freedom elsewhere may in the future transform, and will certainly limit, such sections of European life as are drifting towards the re-establishment of slavery. But the tendency to the re-establishment of slavery as a necessary development of Capitalism is patent wherever Capitalism has power, and nowhere more than in this country.　　　　　　　H. BELLOC.

Kings Land, Shipley,
　Horsham, Sussex,
　　　1913.

INTRODUCTION

THE SUBJECT OF THIS BOOK

INTRODUCTION
THE SUBJECT OF THIS BOOK

THIS BOOK IS WRITTEN TO MAINTAIN and prove the following truth :—

That our free modern society in which the means of production are owned by a few being necessarily in unstable equilibrium, it is tending to reach a condition of stable equilibrium BY THE ESTABLISH-MENT OF COMPULSORY LABOUR LEGALLY ENFORC-IBLE UPON THOSE WHO DO NOT OWN THE MEANS OF PRODUCTION FOR THE ADVANTAGE OF THOSE WHO DO. With this principle of compulsion applied against the non-owners there must also come a differ-ence in their status ; and in the eyes of society and of its positive law men will be divided into two sets : the first economically free and politically free, pos-sessed of the means of production, and securely con-firmed in that possession; the second economically unfree and politically unfree, but at first secured by their very lack of freedom in certain necessaries of life and in a minimum of well-being beneath which they shall not fall.

Society having reached such a condition would be released from its present internal strains and would have taken on a form which would be stable : that is, capable of being indefinitely prolonged without change. In it would be resolved the various factors of instability which increasingly disturb that form of society called *Capitalist*, and men would be satisfied

3

to accept, and to continue in, such a settlement.

To such a stable society I shall give, for reasons which will be described in the next section, the title of THE SERVILE STATE.

I shall not undertake to judge whether this approaching organisation of our modern society be good or evil. I shall concern myself only with showing the necessary tendency towards it which has long existed and the recent social provisions which show that it has actually begun.

This new state will be acceptable to those who desire consciously or by implication the re-establishment among us of a difference of status between possessor and non-possessor : it will be distasteful to those who regard such a distinction with ill favour or with dread.

My business will not be to enter into the discussion between these two types of modern thinkers, but to point out to each and to both that that which the one favours and the other would fly is upon them.

I shall prove my thesis in particular from the case of the industrial society of Great Britain, including that small, alien, and exceptional corner of Ireland, which suffers or enjoys industrial conditions to-day.

I shall divide the matter thus :—

(1) I shall lay down certain definitions.

(2) Next, I shall describe the institution of slavery and THE SERVILE STATE of which it is the basis, as

4

these were in the ancient world.

I shall then:

(3) Sketch very briefly the process whereby that age-long institution of slavery was slowly dissolved during the Christian centuries, and whereby the resulting mediæval system, based upon highly divided property in the means of production, was

(4) wrecked in certain areas of Europe as it approached completion, and had substituted for it, in practice though not in legal theory, a society based upon CAPITALISM.

(5) Next, I shall show how Capitalism was of its nature unstable, because its social realities were in conflict with all existing or possible systems of law, and because its effects in denying *sufficiency* and *security* were intolerable to men; how being thus *unstable*, it consequently presented a *problem* which demanded a solution: to wit, the establishment of some stable form of society whose law and social practice should correspond, and whose economic results, by providing *sufficiency* and *security*, should be tolerable to human nature.

(6) I shall next present the only three possible solutions:—

(*a*) Collectivism, or the placing of the means of production in the hands of the political officers of the community.

(*b*) Property, or the re-establishment of a Distributive State in which the mass of citizens should severally own the means of production.

(*c*) Slavery, or a Servile State in which those who do not own the means of production shall be legally compelled to work for those who do, and shall receive in exchange a security of livelihood.

Now, seeing the distaste which the remains of our long Christian tradition have bred in us for directly advocating the third solution and boldly supporting the re-establishment of slavery, the first two alone are open to reformers: (1) a reaction towards a condition of well-divided property or the *Distributive State*; (2) an attempt to achieve the ideal *Collectivist State*.

It can easily be shown that this second solution appeals most naturally and easily to a society already Capitalist on account of the difficulty which such a society has to discover the energy, the will, and the vision requisite for the first solution.

(7) I shall next proceed to show how the pursuit of this ideal Collectivist State which is bred of Capitalism leads men acting upon a Capitalist society *not* towards the Collectivist State nor anything like it, but to that third utterly different thing—the *Servile State*.

To this eighth section I shall add an appendix showing how the attempt to achieve Collectivism gradually by public purchase is based upon an illusion.

(8) Recognising that theoretical argument of this kind, though intellectually convincing, is not suffi-

6

cient to the establishment of my thesis, I shall conclude by giving examples from modern English legislation, which examples prove that the Servile State
is actually upon us.

Such is the scheme I design for this book.

SECTION ONE
DEFINITIONS

SECTION THE FIRST   DEFINITIONS

MAN, LIKE EVERY OTHER ORGANISM, can only live by the transformation of his environment to his own use. He must transform his environment from a condition where it is less to a condition where it is more subservient to his needs.

That special, conscious, and intelligent transformation of his environment which is peculiar to the peculiar intelligence and creative faculty of man we call the *Production of Wealth*.

Wealth is matter which has been consciously and intelligently transformed from a condition in which it is less to a condition in which it is more serviceable to a human need.

Without *Wealth* man cannot exist. The production of it is a necessity to him, and though it proceeds from the more to the less necessary, and even to those forms of production which we call luxuries, yet in any given human society there is a certain *kind* and a certain *amount* of wealth without which human life cannot be lived : as, for instance, in England to-day, certain forms of elaborately prepared food, clothing, fuel, and habitation.

Therefore, to control the production of wealth is to control human life itself. To refuse man the opportunity for the production of wealth is to refuse him the opportunity for life; and, in general, the way in which the production of wealth is by law permitted is the only way in which the citizens can legally exist.

11

THE SERVILE STATE

Wealth can only be produced by the application of human energy, mental and physical, to the forces of nature around us, and to the material which those forces inform.

This human energy so applicable to the material world and its forces we will call *Labour*. As for that material and those natural forces, we will call them, for the sake of shortness, by the narrow, but conventionally accepted, term *Land*.

It would seem, therefore, that all problems connected with the production of wealth, and all discussion thereupon, involve but two principal original factors, to wit, *Labour* and *Land*. But it so happens that the conscious, artificial, and intelligent action of man upon nature, corresponding to his peculiar character compared with other created beings, introduces a third factor of the utmost importance.

Man proceeds to create wealth by ingenious methods of varying and often increasing complexity, and aids himself by the construction of *implements*. These soon become in each new department of the production as truly necessary to that production as *labour* and *land*. Further, any process of production takes a certain time; during that time the producer must be fed, and clothed, and housed, and the rest of it. There must therefore be an *accumulation of wealth* created in the past, and reserved with the object of maintaining labour during its effort to produce for the future.

DEFINITIONS

Whether it be the making of an instrument or tool, or the setting aside of a store of provisions, *labour* applied to *land* for either purpose is not producing wealth for immediate consumption. It is setting aside and reserving somewhat, and that *somewhat* is always necessary in varying proportions according to the simplicity or complexity of the economic society to the production of wealth.

To such wealth reserved and set aside for the purposes of future production, and not for immediate consumption, whether it be in the form of instruments and tools, or in the form of stores for the maintenance of labour during the process of production, we give the name of *Capital*.

There are thus three factors in the production of all human wealth, which we may conventionally term *Land, Capital*, and *Labour*.

When we talk of the *Means of Production* we signify land and capital combined. Thus, when we say that a man is " dispossessed of the means of production," or cannot produce wealth save by the leave of another who "possesses the means of production," we mean that he is the master only of his labour and has no control, in any useful amount, over either capital, or land, or both combined.

A man politically free, that is, one who enjoys the right before the law to exercise his energies when he pleases (or not at all if he does not so please),

13

but not possessed by legal right of control over any useful amount of the means of production, we call *proletarian*, and any considerable class composed of such men we call a *proletariat*.

Property is a term used for that arrangement in society whereby the control of land and of wealth made from land, including therefore all the means of production, is vested in some person or corporation. Thus we may say of a building, including the land upon which it stands, that it is the " property " of such and such a citizen, or family, or college, or of the State, meaning that those who " own " such property are guaranteed by the laws in the right to use it or withhold it from use. *Private property* signifies such wealth (including the means of production) as may, by the arrangements of society, be in the control of persons or corporations *other* than the political bodies of which these persons or corporations are in another aspect members. What distinguishes private property is not that the possessor thereof is less than the State, or is only a part of the State (for were that so we should talk of municipal property as private property), but rather that the owner may exercise his control over it to his own advantage, and not as a trustee for society, nor in the hierarchy of political institutions. Thus Mr Jones is a citizen of Manchester, but he does not own his private property as a citizen of Manchester, he owns

14

DEFINITIONS

it as Mr Jones, whereas, if the house next to his own be owned by the Manchester municipality, they own it only because they are a political body standing for the whole community of the town. Mr Jones might move to Glasgow and still own his property in Manchester, but the municipality of Manchester can only own its property in connection with the corporate political life of the town.

An ideal society in which the means of production should be in the hands of the political officers of the community we call *Collectivist*, or more generally *Socialist*.*

A society in which private property in land and capital, that is, the ownership and therefore the control of the means of production, is confined to some number of free citizens not large enough to determine the social mass of the State, while the rest have not such property and are therefore proletarian, we call *Capitalist*; and the method by which wealth is produced in such a society can only be the application of labour, the determining mass of which must necessarily be proletarian, to land and capital, in such fashion that, of the total wealth produced, the Proletariat which labours shall only receive a portion.

The two marks, then, defining the Capitalist State

* Save in this special sense of "Collectivist," the word "Socialist" has either no clear meaning, or is used synonymously with other older and better-known words.

are: (1) That the citizens thereof are politically free: *i.e.* can use or withhold at will their possessions or their labour, but are also (2) divided into capitalist and proletarian in such proportions that the State as a whole is not characterised by the institution of ownership among free citizens, but by the restriction of ownership to a section markedly less than the whole, or even to a small minority. Such a *Capitalist State* is essentially divided into two classes of free citizens, the one capitalist or owning, the other propertyless or proletarian.

My last definition concerns the Servile State itself, and since the idea is both somewhat novel and also the subject of this book, I will not only establish but expand its definition.

The definition of the Servile State is as follows:—

" *That arrangement of society in which so considerable a number of the families and individuals are constrained by positive law to labour for the advantage of other families and individuals as to stamp the whole community with the mark of such labour we call* THE SERVILE STATE."

Note first certain negative limitations in the above which must be clearly seized if we are not to lose clear thinking in a fog of metaphor and rhetoric.

That society is not servile in which men are intelligently constrained to labour by enthusiasm, by a religious tenet, or indirectly from fear of destitu-

DEFINITIONS

tion, or directly from love of gain, or from the common sense which teaches them that by their labour they may increase their well-being.

A clear boundary exists between the servile and the non-servile condition of labour, and the conditions upon either side of that boundary utterly differ one from another. Where there is *compulsion* applicable by *positive law* to men of a certain *status*, and such compulsion enforced in the last resort by the powers at the disposal of the State, there is the institution of *Slavery*; and if that institution be sufficiently expanded the whole State may be said to repose upon a servile basis, and is a Servile State.

Where such formal, legal status is absent the conditions are not servile; and the difference between servitude and freedom, appreciable in a thousand details of actual life, is most glaring in this: that the free man can refuse his labour and use that refusal as an instrument wherewith to *bargain*; while the slave has no such instrument or power to bargain at all, but is dependent for his well-being upon the custom of society, backed by the regulation of such of its laws as may protect and guarantee the slave.

Next, let it be observed that the State is not servile because the mere institution of slavery is to be discovered somewhere within its confines. The State is only servile when so considerable a body of forced labour is affected by the compulsion of positive law

17

as to give a character to the whole community.

Similarly, that State is not servile in which *all* citizens are liable to submit their energies to the compulsion of positive law, and must labour at the discretion of State officials. By loose metaphor and for rhetorical purposes men who dislike Collectivism (for instance) or the discipline of a regiment will talk of the "servile" conditions of such organisations. But for the purposes of strict definition and clear thinking it is essential to remember that a servile condition only exists by contrast with a free condition. The servile condition is present in society only when there is also present the free citizen for whose benefit the slave works under the compulsion of positive law.

Again, it should be noted that this word "servile" in no way connotes the worst, nor even necessarily a bad, arrangement of society. This point is so clear that it should hardly delay us; but a confusion between the rhetorical and the precise use of the word servile I have discovered to embarrass public discussion of the matter so much that I must once more emphasise what should be self-evident.

The discussion as to whether the institution of slavery be a good or a bad one, or be relatively better or worse than other alternative institutions, has nothing whatever to do with the exact definition of that institution. Thus Monarchy consists in throwing the

18

DEFINITIONS

responsibility for the direction of society upon an individual. One can imagine some Roman of the first century praising the new Imperial power, but through a muddle-headed tradition against "kings" swearing that he would never tolerate a "monarchy." Such a fellow would have been a very futile critic of public affairs under Trajan, but no more futile than a man who swears that nothing shall make him a "slave," though well prepared to accept laws that compel him to labour without his consent, under the force of public law, and upon terms dictated by others.

Many would argue that a man so compelled to labour, guaranteed against insecurity and against insufficiency of food, housing and clothing, promised subsistence for his old age, and a similar set of advantages for his posterity, would be a great deal better off than a free man lacking all these things. But the argument does not affect the definition attaching to the word servile. A devout Christian of blameless life drifting upon an ice-floe in the Arctic night, without food or any prospect of succour, is not so comfortably circumstanced as the Khedive of Egypt; but it would be folly in establishing the definition of the words "Christian" and "Mahommedan" to bring this contrast into account.

We must then, throughout this inquiry, keep strictly to the economic aspect of the case. Only when that is established and when the modern tendency

19

to the re-establishment of slavery is clear, are we free to discuss the advantages and disadvantages of the revolution through which we are passing.

It must further be grasped that the essential mark of the Servile Institution does not depend upon the ownership of the slave by a particular master. That the institution of slavery tends to that form under the various forces composing human nature and human society is probable enough. That if or when slavery were re-established in England a particular man would in time be found the slave not of Capitalism in general but of, say, the Shell Oil Trust in particular, is a very likely development; and we know that in societies where the institution was of immemorial antiquity such direct possession of the slave by the free man or corporation of free men had come to be the rule. But my point is that such a mark is not essential to the character of slavery. As an initial phase in the institution of slavery, or even as a permanent phase marking society for an indefinite time, it is perfectly easy to conceive of a whole class rendered servile by positive law, and compelled by such law to labour for the advantage of another non-servile free class, without any direct act of possession permitted to one man over the person of another.

The final contrast thus established between slave and free might be maintained by the State guaranteeing to the *un-free*, security in their subsistence, to

DEFINITIONS

the *free*, security in their property and profits, rent and interest. What would mark the slave in such a society would be his belonging to that set or status which was compelled by no matter what definition to labour, and was thus cut off from the other set or status not compelled to labour, but free to labour or not as it willed.

Again, the Servile State would certainly exist even though a man, being only compelled to labour during a portion of his time, were free to bargain and even to accumulate in his " free " time. The old lawyers used to distinguish between a serf " in gross " and a serf " regardant." A serf " in gross " was one who was a serf at all times and places, and not in respect to a particular lord. A serf " regardant " was a serf only in his bondage to serve a particular lord. He was free as against other men. And one might perfectly well have slaves who were only slaves " regardant " to a particular type of employment during particular hours. But they would be slaves none the less, and if their hours were many and their class numerous, the State which they supported would be a Servile State.

Lastly, let it be remembered that the servile condition remains as truly an institution of the State when it attaches permanently and irrevocably at any one time to a set *condition* of human beings as when it attaches to a particular class throughout their lives.

21

THE SERVILE STATE

Thus the laws of Paganism permitted the slave to be enfranchised by his master: it further permitted children or prisoners to be sold into slavery. The Servile Institution, though perpetually changing in the elements of its composition, was still an unchanging factor in the State. Similarly, though the State should only subject to slavery those who had less than a certain income, while leaving men free to pass by inheritance or otherwise out of, and by loss to pass into, the slave class, that slave class, though fluctuating as to its composition, would still permanently exist.

Thus, if the modern industrial State shall make a law by which servile conditions shall not attach to those capable of earning more than a certain sum by their own labour, but shall attach to those who earn less than this sum ; or if the modern industrial State defines manual labour in a particular fashion, renders it compulsory during a fixed time for those who undertake it, but leaves them free to turn later to other occupations if they choose, undoubtedly such distinctions, though they attach to *conditions* and not to a *class*, establish the Servile Institution.

Some considerable number must be manual workers by definition, and while they were so defined would be slaves. Here again the composition of the Servile group would fluctuate, but the institution would be fixed and large enough to stamp all society. I need

22

not insist upon the practical effect: that such a condition, once established, tends to permanence in the great majority of those who suffer it, and that the individuals entering or leaving servitude tend to become few compared to the whole mass.

There is one last point to be considered in this definition.

It is this :—

Since, in the nature of things, a free society must enforce a contract (a free society consisting in nothing else but the enforcement of free contracts), how far can that be called a Servile condition which is the result of contract nominally or really free? In other words, is not a contract to labour, however freely entered into, servile of its nature when enforced by the State?

For instance, I have no food or clothing, nor do I possess the means of production whereby I can produce any wealth in exchange for such. I am so circumstanced that an owner of the Means of Production will not allow me access to those Means unless I sign a contract to serve him for a week at a wage of bare subsistence. Does the State in enforcing that contract make me for that week a slave?

Obviously not. For the institution of Slavery presupposes a certain attitude of mind in the free man and in the slave, a habit of living in either, and the stamp of both those habits upon society. No such

23

effects are produced by a contract enforceable to the length of one week. The duration of human life is such, and the prospect of posterity, that the fulfilling of such a contract in no way wounds the senses of liberty and of choice.

What of a month, a year, ten years, a lifetime? Suppose an extreme case, and a destitute man to sign a contract binding him and all his children who were minors to work for a bare subsistence until his own death, or the attainment of majority of the children, whichever event might happen latest; would the State in enforcing that contract be making the man a slave?

As undoubtedly as it would not be making him a slave in the first case, it would be making him a slave in the second.

One can only say to ancient sophistical difficulties of this kind, that the sense of men establishes for itself the true limits of any object, as of freedom. What freedom is, or is not, in so far as mere measure of time is concerned (though of course much else than time enters in), human habit determines; but the enforcing of a contract of service certainly or probably leaving a choice after its expiration is consonant with freedom. The enforcement of a contract probably binding one's whole life is not consonant with freedom. One binding to service a man's natural heirs is intolerable to freedom.

DEFINITIONS

Consider another converse point. A man binds himself to work for life and his children after him so far as the law may permit him to bind them in a particular society, but that not for a bare subsistence, but for so large a wage that he will be wealthy in a few years, and his posterity, when the contract is completed, wealthier still. Does the State in forcing such a contract make the fortunate employee a slave? No. For it is in the essence of slavery that subsistence or little more than subsistence should be guaranteed to the slave. Slavery exists in order that the Free should benefit by its existence, and connotes a condition in which the men subjected to it may demand secure existence, but little more.

If anyone were to draw an exact line, and to say that a life-contract enforceable by law was slavery at so many shillings a week, but ceased to be slavery after that margin, his effort would be folly. None the less, there is a standard of subsistence in any one society, the guarantee of which (or little more) under an obligation to labour by compulsion is slavery, while the guarantee of very much more is not slavery.

This verbal jugglery might be continued. It is a type of verbal difficulty apparent in every inquiry open to the professional disputant, but of no effect upon the mind of the honest inquirer whose business is not dialectic but truth.

It is always possible by establishing a cross-section in a set of definitions to pose the unanswerable difficulty of degree, but that will never affect the realities of discussion. We know, for instance, what is meant by torture when it exists in a code of laws, and when it is forbidden. No imaginary difficulties of degree between pulling a man's hair and scalping him, between warming him and burning him alive, will disturb a reformer whose business it is to expunge torture from some penal code.

In the same way we know what is and what is not compulsory labour, what is and what is not the Servile Condition. Its test is, I repeat, the withdrawal from a man of his free choice to labour or not to labour, here or there, for such and such an object; and the compelling of him by positive law to labour for the advantage of others who do not fall under the same compulsion.

Where you have *that*, you have slavery : with all the manifold, spiritual, and political results of that ancient institution.

Where you have slavery affecting a class of such considerable size as to mark and determine the character of the State, there you have the Servile State.

To sum up, then:—The SERVILE STATE is that in which we find so considerable a body of families and individuals distinguished from *free citizens* by the mark of compulsory labour as to stamp a general

DEFINITIONS

character upon society, and all the chief characters, good or evil, attaching to the institution of slavery will be found permeating such a State, whether the slaves be directly and personally attached to their masters, only indirectly attached through the medium of the State, or attached in a third manner through their subservience to corporations or to particular industries. The slave so compelled to labour will be one dispossessed of the means of production, and compelled by law to labour for the advantage of all or any who are possessed thereof. And the distinguishing mark of the slave proceeds from the special action upon him of a positive law which separates within the general body of the community one body of men, the less-free, from another, the more-free, in the function of contract.

Now, from a purely Servile conception of production and of the arrangement of society we Europeans sprang. The Immemorial past of Europe is a Servile past. During some centuries which the Church raised, permeated, and constructed, Europe was gradually released or divorced from this immemorial and fundamental conception of slavery; to that conception, to that institution, our Industrial or Capitalist society is now upon its return. We are re-establishing the slave.

Before proceeding to the proof of this, I shall, in

the next few pages, digress to sketch very briefly the process whereby the old Pagan slavery was transformed into a free society some centuries ago. I shall then outline the further process whereby the new non-servile society was wrecked at the Reformation in certain areas of Europe, and particularly in England. There was gradually produced in its stead the transitory phase of society (now nearing its end) called generally *Capitalism* or the *Capitalist State*.

Such a digression, being purely historical, is not logically necessary to a consideration of our subject, but it is of great value to the reader, because the knowledge of how, in reality and in the concrete, things have moved better enables us to understand the logical process whereby they tend towards a particular goal in the future.

One could prove the tendency towards the Servile State in modern England to a man who knew nothing of the past of Europe; but that tendency will seem to him far more reasonably probable, far more a matter of experience and less a matter of mere deduction, when he knows what our society once was, and how it changed into what we know to-day.

SECTION TWO

OUR CIVILISATION WAS ORIGINALLY SERVILE

SECTION TWO   OUR CIVIL-
ISATION WAS ORIGINALLY SERVILE

IN NO MATTER WHAT FIELD OF THE
European past we make our research, we find, from
two thousand years ago upwards, one fundamental
institution whereupon the whole of society reposes;
that fundamental institution is Slavery.

There is here no distinction between the highly
civilised City-State of the Mediterranean, with its
letters, its plastic art, and its code of laws, with all
that makes a civilisation—and this stretching back far
beyond any surviving record,—there is here no distinction between that civilised body and the Northern
and Western societies of the Celtic tribes, or of the
little known hordes that wandered in the Germanies.
All indifferently reposed upon slavery. It was a fundamental conception of society. It was everywhere
present, nowhere disputed.

There *is* a distinction (or would appear to be) between Europeans and Asiatics in this matter. The
religion and morals of the one so differed in their
very origin from those of the other that every social
institution was touched by the contrast—and Slavery
among the rest.

But with that we need not concern ourselves. My
point is that our European ancestry, those men from
whom we are descended and whose blood runs with
little admixture in our veins, took slavery for granted,
made of it the economic pivot upon which the pro-

31

duction of wealth should turn, and never doubted but that it was normal to all human society.

It is a matter of capital importance to seize this.

An arrangement of such a sort would not have endured without intermission(and indeed without question) for many centuries, nor have been found emerging fully grown from that vast space of unrecorded time during which barbarism and civilisation flourished side by side in Europe, had there not been something in it, good or evil, native to our blood.

There was no question in those ancient societies from which we spring of making subject races into slaves by the might of conquering races. All that is the guess-work of the universities. Not only is there no proof of it, rather all the existing proof is the other way. The Greek had a Greek slave, the Latin a Latin slave, the German a German slave, the Celt a Celtic slave. The theory that "superior races" invading a land either drove out the original inhabitants or reduced them to slavery, is one which has no argument either from our present knowledge of man's mind or from recorded evidence. Indeed, the most striking feature of that Servile Basis upon which Paganism reposed was the human equality recognised between master and slave. The master might kill the slave, but both were of one race and each was human to the other.

This spiritual value was not, as a further pernicious

OUR SERVILE CIVILISATION

piece of guess-work would dream, a "growth" or a "progress." The doctrine of human equality was inherent in the very stuff of antiquity, as it is still inherent in societies which have not lost tradition.

We may presume that the barbarian of the North would grasp the great truth with less facility than the civilised man of the Mediterranean, because barbarism everywhere shows a retrogression in intellectual power; but the proof that the Servile Institution was a social arrangement rather than a distinction of type is patent from the coincidence everywhere of Emancipation with Slavery. Pagan Europe not only thought the existence of Slaves a natural necessity to society, but equally thought that upon giving a Slave his freedom the enfranchised man would naturally step, though perhaps after the interval of some lineage, into the ranks of free society. Great poets and great artists, statesmen and soldiers were little troubled by the memory of a servile ancestry.

On the other hand, there was a perpetual recruitment of the Servile Institution, just as there was a perpetual emancipation from it, proceeding year after year; and the natural or normal method of recruitment is most clearly apparent to us in the simple and barbaric societies which the observation of contemporary civilised Pagans enables us to judge.

It was poverty that made the slave.

Prisoners of war taken in set combat afforded one

mode of recruitment, and there was also the raiding of men by pirates in the outer lands and the selling of them in the slave markets of the South. But at once the cause of the recruitment and the permanent support of the institution of slavery was the indigence of the man who sold himself into slavery, *or was born into it*; for it was a rule of Pagan Slavery that the slave bred the slave, and that even if one of the parents were free the offspring was a slave.

The society of antiquity, therefore, was normally divided (as must at last be the society of any servile state) into clearly marked sections: there was upon the one hand the citizen who had a voice in the conduct of the State, who would often labour—but labour of his own free will—and who was normally possessed of property; upon the other hand, there was a mass dispossessed of the means of production and compelled by positive law to labour at command.

It is true that in the further developments of society the accumulation of private savings by a slave was tolerated and that slaves so favoured did sometimes purchase their freedom.

It is further true that in the confusion of the last generations of Paganism there arose in some of the great cities a considerable class of men who, though free, were dispossessed of the means of production. But these last never existed in a sufficient proportion to stamp the whole State of society with a char-

OUR SERVILE CIVILISATION

acter drawn from their proletarian circumstance. To the end the Pagan world remained a world of free proprietors possessed, in various degrees, of the land and of the capital whereby wealth may be produced, and applying to that land and capital for the purpose of producing wealth, *compulsory* labour.

Certain features in that original Servile State from which we all spring should be carefully noted by way of conclusion.

First, though all nowadays contrast slavery with freedom to the advantage of the latter, yet men then accepted slavery freely as an alternative to indigence.

Secondly (and this is most important for our judgment of the Servile Institution as a whole, and of the chances of its return), in all those centuries we find no organised effort, nor (what is still more significant) do we find any *complaint of conscience* against the institution which condemned the bulk of human beings to forced labour.

Slaves may be found in the literary exercises of the time bewailing their lot—and joking about it ; some philosophers will complain that an ideal society should contain no slaves ; others will excuse the establishment of slavery upon this plea or that, while granting that it offends the dignity of man. The greater part will argue of the State that it is necessarily Servile. But no one, slave or free, dreams of abolishing or even of changing the thing. You have no martyrs for

35

the case of " freedom " as against " slavery." The so-called Servile wars are the resistance on the part of escaped slaves to any attempt at recapture, but they are not accompanied by an accepted affirmation that servitude is an intolerable thing; nor is that note struck at all from the unknown beginnings to the Catholic endings of the Pagan world. Slavery is irksome, undignified, woeful ; but it is, to them, of the nature of things.

You may say, to be brief, that this arrangement of society was the very air which Pagan Antiquity breathed.

Its great works, its leisure and its domestic life, its humour, its reserves of power, all depend upon the fact that its society was that of the Servile State.

Men were happy in that arrangement, or, at least, as happy as men ever are.

The attempt to escape by a personal effort, whether of thrift, of adventure, or of flattery to a master, from the Servile condition had never even so much of driving power behind it as the attempt many show to-day to escape from the rank of wage-earners to those of employers. Servitude did not seem a hell into which a man would rather die than sink, or out of which at any sacrifice whatsoever a man would raise himself. It was a condition accepted by those who suffered it as much as by those who enjoyed it, and a perfectly necessary part of all that men did and thought

OUR SERVILE CIVILISATION

You find no barbarian from some free place astonished at the institution of Slavery ; you find no Slave pointing to a society in which Slavery was unknown as towards a happier land. To our ancestors not only for those few centuries during which we have record of their actions, but apparently during an illimitable past, the division of society into those who must work under compulsion and those who would benefit by their labour was the very plan of the State—apart from which they could hardly think of society as existing at all.

Let all this be clearly grasped. It is fundamental to an understanding of the problem before us. Slavery is no novel experience in the history of Europe; nor is one suffering an odd dream when one talks of Slavery as acceptable to European men. Slavery was of the very stuff of Europe for thousands upon thousands of years, until Europe engaged upon that considerable moral experiment called *The Faith*, which many believe to be now accomplished and discarded, and in the failure of which it would seem that the old and primary institution of Slavery must return.

For there came upon us Europeans, after all those centuries, and centuries of a settled social order which was erected upon Slavery as upon a sure foundation, the experiment called the Christian Church.

Among the by-products of this experiment, very slowly emerging from the old Pagan world, and not

THE SERVILE STATE

long completed before Christendom itself suffered a shipwreck, was the exceedingly gradual transformation of the Servile State into something other: a society of owners. And how that something other did proceed from the Pagan Servile State I will next explain.

SECTION THREE

HOW THE SERVILE INSTITU-
TION WAS FOR A TIME
DISSOLVED

THE PROCESS BY WHICH SLAVERY
disappeared among Christian men, though very lengthy in its development (it covered close upon a thousand years), and though exceedingly complicated in
its detail, may be easily and briefly grasped in its main
lines.

Let it first be clearly understood that the vast revolution through which the European mind passed
between the first and the fourth centuries (that revolution which is often termed the Conversion of the World
to Christianity, but which should for purposes of historical accuracy be called the Growth of the Church)
included no attack upon the Servile Institution.

No dogma of the Church pronounced Slavery to
be immoral, or the sale and purchase of men to be a
sin, or the imposition of compulsory labour upon a
Christian to be a contravention of any human right.

The emancipation of Slaves was indeed regarded
as a good work by the Faithful: but so was it regarded
by the Pagan. It was, on the face of it, a service rendered to one's fellowmen. The sale of Christians to
Pagan masters was abhorrent to the later empire of
the Barbarian Invasions, not because slavery in itself
was condemned, but because it was a sort of treason
to civilisation to force men away from Civilisation to
Barbarism. In general you will discover no pronounce-

ment against slavery as an institution, nor any moral
definition attacking it, throughout all those early
Christian centuries during which it none the less
effectively disappears.

The form of its disappearance is well worth noting.
It begins with the establishment as the fundamental
unit of production in Western Europe of those great
landed estates, commonly lying in the hands of a single
proprietor, and generally known as VILLÆ.

There were, of course, many other forms of human
agglomeration: small peasant farms owned in absolute proprietorship by their petty masters; groups of
free men associated in what was called a *Vicus*; manu-
factories in which groups of slaves were industrially
organised to the profit of their master; and, governing the regions around them, the scheme of Roman
towns.

But of all these the *Villa* was the dominating type;
and as society passed from the high civilisation of
the first four centuries into the simplicity of the Dark
Ages, the *Villa*, the unit of agricultural production,
became more and more the model of all society.

Now the *Villa* began as a considerable extent of
land, containing, like a modern English estate, pasture,
arable, water, wood and heath, or waste land. It was
owned by a *dominus* or *lord* in absolute proprietorship,
to sell, or leave by will, to do with it whatsoever he
chose. It was cultivated for him by *Slaves* to whom

42

he owed nothing in return, and whom it was simply his interest to keep alive and to continue breeding in order that they might perpetuate his wealth.

I concentrate particularly upon these Slaves, the great majority of the human beings inhabiting the land, because, although there arose in the Dark Ages, when the Roman Empire was passing into the society of the Middle Ages, other social elements within the *Villæ*—the Freed men who owed the lord a modified service, and even occasionally independent citizens present through a contract terminable and freely entered into—yet it is the *Slave* who is the mark of all that society.

At its origin, then, the Roman *Villa* was a piece of absolute property, the production of wealth upon which was due to the application of slave labour to the natural resources of the place; and that slave labour was as much the property of the lord as was the land itself.

The first modification which this arrangement showed in the new society which accompanied the growth and establishment of the Church in the Roman world, was a sort of customary rule which modified the old arbitrary position of the Slave.

The Slave was still a Slave, but it was both more convenient in the decay of communications and public power, and more consonant with the social spirit of the time to make sure of that Slave's produce by asking him for no more than certain customary dues. The Slave and his descendants became more or less rooted to one spot. Some were still bought and sold, but in decreasing numbers. As the generations passed a larger and a larger proportion lived where and as their fathers had lived, and the produce which they raised was fixed more and more at a certain amount, which the lord was content to receive and ask no more. The arrangement was made workable by leaving to the Slave all the remaining produce of his own labour. There was a sort of implied bargain here, in the absence of public powers and in the decline of the old highly centralised and vigorous system which could always guarantee to the master the full product of the Slave's effort. The bargain implied was, that if the Slave Community of the *Villa* would produce for the benefit of its Lord not less than a certain customary amount of goods from the soil of the *Villa*, the Lord could count on their always exercising that effort by leaving to them all the surplus, which they could increase, if they willed, indefinitely.

By the ninth century, when this process had been gradually at work for a matter of some three hundred years, one fixed form of productive unit began to be apparent throughout Western Christendom.

The old absolutely owned estate had come to be divided into three portions. One of these was pasture and arable land, reserved privately to the lord, and called *domain* : that is, lord's land. Another was in the occupation, and already almost in the possession (practically, though not legally), of those who had once been Slaves. A third was common land over which both the Lord and the Slave exercised each their various rights, which rights were minutely remembered and held sacred by custom. For instance, in a certain village, if there was beech pasture for three hundred swine, the lord might put in but fifty : two hundred and fifty were the rights of the " village."

Upon the first of these portions, Domain, wealth was produced by the obedience of the Slave for certain fixed hours of labour. He must come so many days a week, or upon such and such occasions (all fixed and customary), to till the land of the Domain for his Lord, and *all* the produce of this must be handed over to the Lord—though, of course, a daily wage in kind was allowed, for the labourer must live.

Upon the second portion, " Land in Villenage," which was nearly always the most of the arable and pasture land of the *Villæ*, the Slaves worked by rules and customs which they gradually came to elaborate for themselves. They worked under an officer of their own, sometimes nominated, sometimes elected: nearly always, in practice, a man suitable to them and more or less of their choice ; though this co-operative work upon the old Slave-ground was controlled by the general customs of the village, common to lord and slave alike, and the principal officer over both kinds of land was the Lord's Steward.

Of the wealth so produced by the Slaves, a certain fixed portion (estimated originally in kind) was payable to the Lord's Bailiff, and became the property of the Lord.

Finally, on the third division of the land, the "Waste," the "Wood," the "Heath," and certain common pastures, wealth was produced as elsewhere by the labour of those who had once been the Slaves, but divided in customary proportions between them and their master. Thus, such and such a water meadow would have grazing for so many oxen ; the number was rigidly defined, and of that number so many would be the Lord's and so many the Villagers'.

During the eighth, ninth and tenth centuries this system crystallised and became so natural in men's eyes that the original servile character of the working folk upon the *Villa* was forgotten.

The documents of the time are rare. These three centuries are the crucible of Europe, and record is drowned and burnt in them. Our study of their social conditions, especially in the latter part, are matter rather of inference than of direct evidence. But the sale and purchase of men, already exceptional at the beginning of this period, is almost unknown before the end of it. Apart from domestic slaves within the household, slavery in the old sense which Pagan antiquity gave that institution had been transformed out of all knowledge, and when, with the eleventh century, the true Middle Ages begin to spring from the soil of the Dark Ages, and a new civilisation to arise, though the old word *servus* (the Latin for a slave) is still used for the man who works the soil, his status in the now increasing number of documents which we can consult is wholly changed; we can certainly no longer translate the word by the English word *slave*; we are compelled to translate it by a new word with very different connotations : the word *serf*.

The Serf of the early Middle Ages, of the eleventh and early twelfth centuries, of the Crusades and the Norman Conquest, is already nearly a peasant. He is indeed bound in legal theory to the soil upon which he was born. In social practice, all that is required of him is that his family should till its quota of servile land, and that the dues to the lord shall not fail from absence of labour. That duty fulfilled, it is easy and common for members of the serf-class to enter the professions and the Church, or to go wild; to become men practically free in the growing industries of the towns. With every passing generation the ancient servile conception of the labourer's status grows more and more dim, and the Courts and the practice of society treat him more and more as a man strictly bound to certain dues and to certain periodical labour within his industrial unit,

47

but in all other respects free.

As the civilisation of the Middle Ages develops, as wealth increases and the arts progressively flourish, this character of freedom becomes more marked. In spite of attempts in time of scarcity (as after a plague) to insist upon the old rights to compulsory labour, the habit of commuting these rights for money-payments and dues has grown too strong to be resisted.

If at the end of the fourteenth century, let us say, or at the beginning of the fifteenth, you had visited some Squire upon his estate in France or in England, he would have told you of the whole of it, " These are my lands." But the peasant (as he now was) would have said also of his holding, " This is my land." He could not be evicted from it. The dues which he was customarily bound to pay were but a fraction of its total produce. He could not always sell it, but it was always inheritable from father to son ; and, in general, at the close of this long process of a thousand years the Slave had become a free man for all the ordinary purposes of society. He bought and sold. He saved as he willed, he invested, he built, he drained at his discretion, and if he improved the land it was to his own profit.

Meanwhile, side by side with this emancipation of mankind in the direct line of descent from the old chattel slaves of the Roman *villa* went, in the Middle Ages, a crowd of institutions which all similarly made for a distribution of property, and for the destruction of even the fossil remnants of a then forgotten Servile State. Thus industry of every kind in the towns, in transport, in crafts, and in commerce, was organised in the form of *Guilds*. And a Guild was a society partly co-operative, but in the main composed of private owners of capital whose corporation was self-governing, and was designed to check competition between its members : to prevent the growth of one at the expense of the other. Above all, most jealously did the Guild safeguard the division of property, so that there should be formed within its ranks no proletariat upon the one side, and no monopolising capitalist upon the other.

There was a period of apprenticeship at a man's entry into a Guild, during which he worked for a master ; but in time he became a master in his turn. The existence of such corporations as the normal units of industrial production, of commercial effort, and of the means of transport, is proof enough of what the social spirit was which had also enfranchised the labourer upon the land. And while such institutions flourished side by side with the no longer servile village communities, freehold or absolute possession of the soil, as distinguished from the tenure of the serf under the lord, also increased.

These three forms under which labour was exercised—the serf, secure in his position, and burdened only with regular dues, which were but a fraction of his produce; the freeholder, a man independent save for money dues, which were more of a tax than a rent; the Guild, in which well-divided capital worked co-operatively for craft production, for transport and for commerce—all three between them were making for a society which should be based upon the principle of property. All, or most,—the normal family—should own. And on ownership the freedom of the State should repose.

The State, as the minds of men envisaged it at the close of this process, was an agglomeration of families of varying wealth, but by far the greater number owners of the means of production. It was an agglomeration in which the stability of this *distributive* system (as I have called it) was guaranteed by the existence of co-operative bodies, binding men of the same craft or of the same village together; guaranteeing the small proprietor against loss of his economic independence, while at the same time it guaranteed society against the growth of a proletariat. If liberty of purchase and of sale, of mortgage and of inheritance was restricted, it was restricted with the social object of preventing the growth of an economic oligarchy which could exploit the rest of the community. The restraints upon liberty were restraints designed for the preservation of liberty; and every action of Mediæval Society, from the flower of the

THE SERVILE DISSOLVED

Middle Ages to the approach of their catastrophe, was directed towards the establishment of a State in which men should be economically free through the possession of capital and of land.

Save here and there in legal formulæ, or in rare patches isolated and eccentric, the Servile Institution had totally disappeared; nor must it be imagined that anything in the nature of Collectivism had replaced it. There was common land, but it was common land jealously guarded by men who were also personal proprietors of other land. Common property in the village was but one of the forms of property, and was used rather as the fly-wheel to preserve the regularity of the co-operative machine than as a type of holding in any way peculiarly sacred. The Guilds had property in common, but that property was the property necessary to their co-operative life: their Halls, their Funds for Relief, their Religious Endowments. As for the instruments of their trades, those instruments were owned by the individual members, *not* by the guild, save where they were of so expensive a kind as to necessitate a corporate control.

Such was the transformation which had come over European society in the course of ten Christian centuries. Slavery had gone, and in its place had come that establishment of free possession which seemed so normal to men, and so consonant to a happy human life. No particular name was then found for it. To-day, and now that it has disappeared, we must construct an awkward one, and say that the Middle Ages had instinctively conceived and brought into existence the DISTRIBUTIVE STATE.

That excellent consummation of human society passed, as we know, and was in certain Provinces of Europe, but more particularly in Britain, destroyed.

For a society in which the determinant mass of families were owners of capital and of land; for one in which production was regulated by self-governing corporations of small owners; and for one in which the misery and insecurity of a proletariat was unknown, there came to be substituted the dreadful moral anarchy against which all moral effort is now turned, and which goes by the name of *Capitalism*.

How did such a catastrophe come about? Why was it permitted, and upon what historical process did the evil batten? What turned an England economically free into the England which we know to-day, of which at least one-third is indigent, of which nineteen-twentieths are dispossessed of capital and of land, and of which the whole industry and national life is controlled upon its economic side by a few chance directors of millions, a few masters of unsocial and irresponsible monopolies?

The answer most usually given to this fundamental question in our history, and the one most readily accepted, is that this misfortune came about through a material process known as the *Industrial Revolution*. The use of expensive machinery, the concentration of industry and of its implements are imagined to have enslaved, in some blind way, apart from the human will, the action of English mankind.

The explanation is wholly false. No such material cause determined the degradation from which we suffer.

It was the deliberate action of men, evil will in a few and apathy of will among the many, which produced a catastrophe as human in its causes and inception as in its vile effect.

Capitalism was not the growth of the industrial movement, nor of chance material discoveries. A little acquaintance with history and a little straightforwardness in the teaching of it would be enough to prove that.

The Industrial System was a growth proceeding from Capitalism, not its cause. Capitalism was here in England before the Industrial System came into being;—before the use of coal and of the new expensive machinery, and of the concentration of the implements of production in the great towns. Had Capitalism not been present before the Industrial Revolution, that revolution might have proved as beneficent to Englishmen as it has proved maleficent. But Capitalism—that is, the ownership by a few of the springs of life—was present long before the great discoveries came. It warped the effect of these discoveries and new inventions, and it turned them from a good into an evil thing. It was not machinery that lost us our freedom; it was the loss of a free mind.

HOW THE DISTRIBUTIVE STATE FAILED

SECTION THE FOURTH   HOW THE DISTRIBUTIVE STATE FAILED

WITH THE CLOSE OF THE MIDDLE AGES the societies of Western Christendom and England among the rest were economically free.

Property was an institution native to the State and enjoyed by the great mass of its citizens. Co-operative institutions, voluntary regulations of labour, restricted the completely independent use of property by its owners only in order to keep that institution intact and to prevent the absorption of small property by great.

This excellent state of affairs which we had reached after many centuries of Christian development, and in which the old institution of slavery had been finally eliminated from Christendom, did not everywhere survive. In England in particular it was ruined. The seeds of the disaster were sown in the sixteenth century. Its first apparent effects came to light in the seventeenth. During the eighteenth century England came to be finally, though insecurely, established upon a proletarian basis, that is, it had already become a society of rich men possessed of the means of production on the one hand, and a majority dispossessed of those means upon the other. With the nineteenth century the evil plant had come to its maturity, and England had become before the close of that period a purely Capitalist State, the type and model of Capitalism for the whole world; with the means of production tightly held by a very small group of citizens, and the whole determining mass of the nation dispossessed of capital and land, and dispossessed, therefore, in all cases of security, and in many of sufficiency as well. The mass of Englishmen, still possessed of political, lacked more and more the elements of economic, freedom, and were in a worse posture than free citizens have ever found themselves before in the history of Europe.

By what steps did so enormous a catastrophe fall upon us?

The first step in the process consisted in the mishandling of a great economic revolution which marked the sixteenth century. The lands and the accumulated wealth of the monasteries were taken out of the hands of their old possessors with the intention of vesting them in the Crown—but they passed, as a fact, not into the hands of the Crown, but into the hands of an already wealthy section of the community who, after the change was complete, became in the succeeding hundred years the governing power of England.

This is what happened :—

The England of the early sixteenth century, the England over which Henry VIII. inherited his powerful Crown in youth, though it was an England in which the great mass of men owned the land they tilled and the houses in which they dwelt, and the implements with which they worked, was yet an England in which these goods, though widely distributed, were distributed unequally.

Then, as now, the soil and its fixtures were the basis of all wealth, but the proportion between the value of the soil and its fixtures and the value of other means of production (implements, stores of clothing and of subsistence, etc.) was different from what it is now. The land and the fixtures upon it formed a very much larger fraction of the totality of the means of production than they do to-day. They represent to-day not one-half the total means of production of this country; and though they are the necessary foundation for all wealth production, yet our great machines, our stores of food and clothing, our coal and oil, our ships and the rest of it, come to more than the true value of the land and of the fixtures upon the land: they come to more than the arable soil and the pasture, the constructional value of the houses, wharves and docks, and so forth. In the early sixteenth century the land and the fixtures upon it came, upon the contrary, to very much more than all other forms of wealth combined.

Now this form of wealth was here, more than in any other Western European country, already in the hands of a wealthy land-owning class at the end of the Middle Ages.

It is impossible to give exact statistics, because none were gathered, and we can only make general statements based upon inference and research. But, roughly speaking, we may say that of the total value of the land and its fixtures, probably rather more than a quarter, though less than a third, was in the hands of this wealthy class.

The England of that day was mainly agricultural, and consisted of more than four, but less than six million people, and in every agricultural community you would have the Lord, as he was legally called (the squire, as he was already conversationally termed), in possession of more demesne land than in any other country. On the average you found him, I say, owning in this absolute fashion rather more than a quarter, perhaps a third of the land of the village: in the towns the distribution was more even. Sometimes it was a private individual who was in this position, sometimes a corporation, but in every village you would have found this demesne land absolutely owned by the political head of the village, occupying a considerable proportion of its acreage. The rest, though distributed as property among the less fortunate of the population, and carrying with it houses and implements from which they could not be dispossessed, paid certain dues to the Lord, and, what was more, the Lord exercised local justice. This class of wealthy land-owners had been also for now one hundred years the Justices upon whom local administration depended.

THE DISTRIBUTIVE FAILED

There was no reason why this state of affairs should not gradually have led to the rise of the Peasant and the decay of the Lord. That is what happened in France, and it might perfectly well have happened here. A peasantry eager to purchase might have gradually extended their holdings at the expense of the demesne land, and to the distribution of property, which was already fairly complete, there might have been added another excellent element, namely, the more equal possession of that property. But any such process of gradual buying by the small man from the great, such as would seem natural to the temper of us European people, and such as has since taken place nearly everywhere in countries which were left free to act upon their popular instincts, was interrupted in this country by an artificial revolution of the most violent kind. This artificial revolution consisted in the seizing of the monastic lands by the Crown.

It is important to grasp clearly the nature of this operation, for the whole economic future of England was to flow from it.

Of the *demesne* lands, and the power of local administration which they carried with them (a very important feature, as we shall see later), rather more than a quarter were in the hands of the Church ; the Church was therefore the "Lord" of something over 25 per cent., say 28 per cent., or perhaps nearly 30

per cent., of English agricultural communities, and
the overseers of a like proportion of all English agricultural produce. The Church was further the absolute owner in practice of something like 30 per
cent. of the demesne land in the villages, and the re-
ceiver of something like 30 per cent. of the customary dues, etc., paid by the smaller owners to the
greater. All this economic power lay until 1535 in
the hands of Cathedral Chapters, communities of
monks and nuns, educational establishments conducted by the clergy, and so forth.

When the Monastic lands were confiscated by
Henry VIII., not the whole of this vast economic
influence was suddenly extinguished. The secular
clergy remained endowed, and most of the educational establishments, though looted, retained some
revenue; but though the whole 30 per cent. did not
suffer confiscation, something well over 20 per cent.
did, and the revolution effected by this vast operation was by far the most complete, the most sudden,
and the most momentous of any that has taken place
in the economic history of any European people.

It was at first *intended* to retain this great mass of
the means of production in the hands of the Crown:
that must be clearly remembered by any student of
the fortunes of England, and by all who marvel at the
contrast between the old England and the new.

Had that intention been firmly maintained, the

THE DISTRIBUTIVE FAILED

English State and its government would have been the most powerful in Europe.

The Executive (which in those days meant the *King*) would have had a greater opportunity for crushing the resistance of the wealthy, for backing its political power with economic power, and for ordering the social life of its subjects than any other executive in Christendom.

Had Henry VIII. and his successors kept the land thus confiscated, the power of the French Monarchy, at which we are astonished, would have been nothing to the power of the English.

The King of England would have had in his own hands an instrument of control of the most absolute sort. He would presumably have used it, as a strong central government always does, for the weakening of the wealthier classes, and to the indirect advantage of the mass of the people. At any rate, we should have a very different England indeed from the England we know, if the King had held fast to his own after the dissolution of the monasteries.

Now it is precisely here that the capital point in this great revolution appears. *The King failed to keep the lands he had seized.* That class of large landowners which already existed and controlled, as I have said, anything from a quarter to a third of the agricultural values of England, were too strong for the monarchy. They insisted upon land being granted

to themselves, sometimes freely, sometimes for ridi-
culously small sums ; and they were strong enough
in Parliament, and through the local administrative
power they held, to see that their demands were satisfied. Nothing that the Crown let go ever went back
to the Crown, and year after year more and more of
what had once been the monastic land became the absolute possession of the large land-owners.

Observe the effect of this. All over England men
who already held in virtually absolute property from
one-quarter to one-third of the soil and the ploughs
and the barns of a village, became possessed in a
very few years of a further great section of the means
of production, which turned the scale wholly in their
favour. They added to that third a new and extra
fifth. They became at a blow the owners of *half* the
land ! In many centres of capital importance they
had come to own *more* than half the land. They were
in many districts not only the unquestioned superiors,
but the economic masters of the rest of the community. They could buy to the greatest advantage. They
were strictly *competitive*, getting every shilling of due
and of rent where the old clerical landlords had been
customary—leaving much to the tenant. They began to fill the universities, the judiciary. The Crown
less and less decided between great and small. More
and more the great could decide in their own favour.
They soon possessed by these operations the bulk of

the means of production, and they immediately began the process of eating up the small independent men and gradually forming those great estates which, in the course of a few generations, became identical with the village itself. All over England you may notice that the great squires' houses date from this revolution or after it. The manorial house, the house of the local great man as it was in the Middle Ages, survives here and there to show of what immense effect this revolution was. The low timbered place with its steadings and outbuildings, only a larger farmhouse among the other farmhouses, is turned after the Reformation and thenceforward into a palace. Save where great castles (which were only held of the Crown and not owned) made an exception, the pre-Reformation gentry lived as men richer than, but not the masters of, other farmers around them. *After* the Reformation there began to arise all over England those great "country houses" which rapidly became the typical centres of English agricultural life.

The process was in full swing before Henry died. Unfortunately for England, he left as his heir a sickly child, during the six years of whose reign, from 1547 to 1553, the loot went on at an appalling rate. When he died and Mary came to the throne it was nearly completed. A mass of new families had arisen, wealthy out of all proportion to anything which the older England had known, and bound by a common interest to the older families which had joined in the grab. Every single man who sat in Parliament for a country required his price for voting the dissolution of the monasteries ; every single man received it. A list of the members of the Dissolution Parliament is enough to prove this, and, apart from their power in Parliament, this class had a hundred other ways of insisting on their will. The Howards(already of some lineage), the Cavendishes, the Cecils, the Russels, and fifty other new families thus rose upon the ruins of religion ; and the process went steadily on until, about one hundred years after its inception, the whole face of England was changed.

In the place of a powerful Crown disposing of revenues far greater than that of any subject, you had a Crown at its wit's end for money, and dominated by subjects some of whom were its equals in wealth, and who could, especially through the action of Parliament (which they now controlled), do much what they willed with Government.

In other words, by the first third of the seventeenth century, by 1630-40, the economic revolution was finally accomplished, and the new economic reality thrusting itself upon the old traditions of England was a powerful oligarchy of large owners overshadowing an impoverished and dwindled monarchy.

Other causes had contributed to this deplorable result. The change in the value of money had hit the

THE DISTRIBUTIVE FAILED

Crown very hard;* the peculiar history of the Tudor family, their violent passions, their lack of resolution and of any continuous policy, to some extent the character of Charles I. himself, and many another subsidiary cause may be quoted. But the great main fact upon which the whole thing is dependent is the fact that the Monastic Lands, at least a fifth of the wealth of the country, had been transferred to the great land-owners, and that this transference had tipped the scale over entirely in their favour as against the peasantry.

The diminished and impoverished Crown could no longer stand. It fought against the new wealth the struggle of the Civil Wars; it was utterly defeated; and when a final settlement was arrived at in 1660 you have all the realities of power in the hands of a small powerful class of wealthy men, the King still surrounded by the forms and traditions of his old power, but in practice a salaried puppet. And in that social world which underlies all political appearances, the great dominating note was that a few wealthy families had got hold of the bulk of the means

* The purchasing power of money fell during this century to about a third of its original standard. £3 (say) would purchase under Charles I. the necessities which £1 would have purchased under Henry VIII. Nearly all the *receipts* of the Crown were customary. Most of its *expenses* were competitive. It continued to get but £1 where it was gradually compelled to pay out £3.

of production in England, while the same families
exercised all local administrative power and were
moreover the Judges, the Higher Education, the
Church, and the generals. They quite overshadowed
what was left of central government in this country.

Take, as a starting-point for what followed, the
date 1700. By that time more than half of the English
were dispossessed of capital and of land. Not one
man in two, even if you reckon the very small owners,
inhabited a house of which he was the secure possessor, or tilled land from which he could not be turned
off.

Such a proportion may seem to us to-day a wonder-
fully free arrangement, and certainly if nearly one-
half of our population were possessed of the means
of production, we should be in a very different situation from that in which we find ourselves. But the
point to seize is that, though the bad business was
very far from completion in or about the year 1700,
yet by that date England had already become CAPI-
TALIST. She had already permitted a vast section of
her population to become *proletarian*, and it is this
and *not* the so-called " Industrial Revolution," a later
thing, which accounts for the terrible social condition
in which we find ourselves to-day.

How true this is what I still have to say in this
section will prove.

In an England thus already cursed with a very

THE DISTRIBUTIVE FAILED

large proletariat class, and in an England already directed by a dominating Capitalist class, possessing the means of production, there came a great industrial development.

Had that industrial development come upon a people economically free, it would have taken a co-operative form. Coming as it did upon a people which had already largely lost its economic freedom, it took at its very origin a *Capitalist* form, and this form it has retained, expanded, and perfected throughout two hundred years.

It was in England that the Industrial System arose. It was in England that all its traditions and habits were formed ; and because the England in which it arose was already a Capitalist England, modern Industrialism, wherever you see it at work to-day, having spread from England, has proceeded upon the Capitalist model.

It was in 1705 that the first practical steam-engine, Newcomen's, was set to work. The life of a man elapsed before this invention was made, by Watt's introduction of the condenser, into the great instrument of production which has transformed our industry—but in those sixty years all the origins of the Industrial System are to be discovered. It was just before Watt's patent that Hargreaves' spinning-jenny appeared. Thirty years earlier, Abraham Darby of Colebrook Dale, at the end of a long series of experi-

ments which had covered more than a century, smelted
iron-ore successfully with coke. Not twenty years
later, King introduced the flying shuttle, the first
great improvement in the hand-loom; and in general
the period covered by such a life as that of Dr Johnson,
born just after Newcomen's engine was first set working, and dying seventy-four years afterwards, when
the Industrial System was in full blast, covers that
great transformation of England. A man who, as a
child, could remember the last years of Queen Anne,
and who lived to the eve of the French Revolution,
saw passing before his eyes the change which transformed English society and has led it to the expansion and peril in which we see it to-day.

What was the characteristic mark of that half-cen-
tury and more? Why did the new inventions give us
the form of society now known and hated under the
name of Industrial? Why did the vast increase in the
powers of production, in population and in accumulation of wealth, turn the mass of Englishmen into a
poverty-stricken proletariat, cut off the rich from the
rest of the nation, and develop to the full all the evils
which we associate with the Capitalist State?

To that question an answer almost as universal as
it is unintelligent has been given. That answer is
not only unintelligent but false, and it will be my business here to show how false it is. The answer so provided in innumerable text-books, and taken almost

as a commonplace in our universities, is that the new methods of production—the new machinery, the new implements—fatally and of themselves developed a Capitalist State in which a few should own the means of production and the mass should be proletarian. The new instruments, it is pointed out, were on so vastly greater a scale than the old, and were so much more expensive, that the small man could not afford them ; while the rich man, who could afford them, ate up by his competition, and reduced from the position of a small owner to that of a wage-earner, his insufficiently equipped competitor who still attempted to struggle on with the older and cheaper tools. To this (we are told) the advantages of concentration were added in favour of the large owner against the small. Not only were the new instruments expensive almost in proportion to their efficiency, but, especially after the introduction of steam, they were efficient in proportion to their concentration in few places and under the direction of a few men. Under the effect of such false arguments as these we have been taught to believe that the horrors of the Industrial System were a blind and necessary product of material and impersonal forces, and that wherever the steam engine, the power loom, the blast furnace and the rest were introduced, there fatally would soon appear a little group of owners exploiting a vast majority of the dispossessed.

It is astonishing that a statement so unhistorical

should have gained so general a credence. Indeed, were the main truths of English history taught in our schools and universities to-day, were educated men familiar with the determining and major facts of the national past, such follies could never have taken root. The vast growth of the proletariat, the concentration of ownership into the hands of a few owners, and the exploitation by those owners of the mass of the community, had no fatal or necessary connection with the discovery of new and perpetually improving methods of production. The evil proceeded in direct historical sequence, proceeded patently and demonstrably, from the fact that England, the seed-plot of the Industrial System, was *already* captured by a wealthy oligarchy *before* the series of great discoveries began.

Consider in what way the Industrial System developed upon Capitalist lines. Why were a few rich men put with such ease into possession of the new methods? Why was it normal and natural in their eyes and in that of contemporary society that those who produced the new wealth with the new machinery should be proletarian and dispossessed? Simply because the England upon which the new discoveries had come was *already* an England owned as to its soil and accumulations of wealth by a small minority: it was *already* an England in which perhaps half of the whole population was proletarian, and a medium for exploitation ready to hand.

THE DISTRIBUTIVE FAILED

When any one of the new industries was launched it had to be *capitalised*; that is, accumulated wealth from some source or other had to be found which would support labour in the process of production until that process should be complete. Someone must find the corn and the meat and the housing and the clothing by which should be supported, between the extraction of the raw material and the moment when the consumption of the finished article could begin, the human agents which dealt with that raw material and turned it into the finished product. Had property been well distributed, protected by co-operative guilds, fenced round and supported by custom and by the autonomy of great artisan corporations, those accumulations of wealth, necessary for the launching of each new method of production and for each new perfection of it, would have been discovered in the mass of small owners. *Their* corporations, *their* little parcels of wealth combined would have furnished the *capitalisation* required for the new processes, and men already owners would, as one invention succeeded another, have increased the total wealth of the community without disturbing the balance of distribution. There is no conceivable link in reason or in experience which binds the capitalisation of a new process with the idea of a few employing owners and a mass of employed non-owners working at a wage. Such great discoveries coming in a society like that of the thirteenth century would have blest and enriched mankind. Coming upon the diseased moral conditions of the eighteenth century in this country, they proved a curse.

To whom could the new industry turn for capitalisation? The small owner had already largely disappeared. The corporate life and mutual obligations which had supported him and confirmed him in his property had been broken to pieces by no "economic development," but by the deliberate action of the rich. He was ignorant because his schools had been taken from him and the universities closed to him. He was the more ignorant because the common life which once nourished his social sense and the co-operative arrangements which had once been his defence had disappeared. When you sought an accumulation of corn, of clothing, of housing, of fuel as the indispensable preliminary to the launching of your new industry; when you looked round for someone who could find the accumulated wealth necessary for these considerable experiments, you had to turn to the class which had already monopolised the bulk of the means of production in England. The rich men alone could furnish you with those supplies.

Nor was this all. The supplies once found and the adventure "capitalised," that form of human energy which lay best to hand, which was indefinitely exploitable, weak, ignorant, and desperately necessitous, ready to produce for you upon almost any terms, and glad enough if you would only keep it alive, was the existing proletariat which the new plutocracy had created when, in cornering the wealth of the country after the Reformation, they had thrust out the mass of Englishmen from the possession of implements, of houses, and of land.

The rich class, adopting some new process of production for its private gain, worked it upon those lines of mere competition which its avarice had already established. Co-operative tradition was dead. Where would it find its cheapest labour? Obviously among the proletariat—not among the remaining small owners. What class would increase under the new wealth? Obviously the proletariat again, without responsibilities, with nothing to leave to its progeny; and as they swelled the capitalist's gain, they enabled him with increasing power to buy out the small owner and send him to swell by another tributary the proletarian mass.

It was upon this account that the Industrial Revolution, as it is called, took in its very origins the form which has made it an almost unmixed curse for the unhappy society in which it has flourished. The rich, already possessed of the accumulations by which that industrial change could alone be nourished, inherited all its succeeding accumulations of implements and all its increasing accumulations of subsistence. The factory system, starting upon a basis

75

of capitalist and proletariat, grew in the mould which had determined its origins. With every new advance the capitalist looked for proletariat grist to feed the productive mill. Every circumstance of that society, the form in which the laws that governed ownership and profit were cast, the obligations of partners, the relations between "master" and "man," directly made for the indefinite expansion of a subject, formless, wage-earning class controlled by a small body of owners, which body would tend to become smaller and richer still, and to be possessed of power ever greater and greater as the bad business unfolded.

The spread of economic oligarchy was everywhere, and not in industry alone. The great landlords destroyed deliberately and of set purpose and to their own advantage the common rights over common land. The small plutocracy with which they were knit up, and with whose mercantile elements they were now fused, directed everything to its own ends. That strong central government which should protect the community against the rapacity of a few had gone generations before. Capitalism triumphant wielded all the mechanism of legislation and of information too. It still holds them ; and there is not an example of so-called "Social Reform" to-day which is not demonstrably (though often subconsciously) directed to the further entrenchment and confirmation of an industrial society in which it is taken for granted that a few shall own, that the vast majority shall live at a wage under them, and that all the bulk of Englishmen may hope for is the amelioration of their lot by regulations and by control from above—but not by property; not by freedom.

We all feel—and those few of us who have analysed the matter not only feel but know—that the Capitalist society thus gradually developed from its origins in the capture of the land four hundred years ago has reached its term. It is almost self-evident that it cannot continue in the form which now three generations have known, and it is equally self-evident that some solution must be found for the intolerable and increasing instability with which it has poisoned our lives. But before considering the solutions variously presented by various schools of thought, I shall in my next section show how and why the English Capitalist Industrial System is thus intolerably unstable and consequently presents an acute problem which must be solved under pain of social death.

It must be noted that modern Industrialism has spread to many other centres from England. It bears everywhere the features stamped upon it by its origin in this country.

THE CAPITALIST STATE IN PROPORTION AS IT GROWS PERFECT GROWS UNSTABLE

SECTION THE FIFTH · THE CAP-ITALIST STATE IN PROPORTION AS IT GROWS PERFECT GROWS UNSTABLE

FROM THE HISTORICAL DIGRESSION which I have introduced by way of illustrating my subject in the last two sections I now return to the general discussion of my thesis and to the logical process by which it may be established.

The Capitalist State is unstable, and indeed more properly a transitory phase lying between two permanent and stable states of society.

In order to appreciate why this is so, let us recall the definition of the Capitalist State:—

"A society in which the ownership of the means of production is confined to a body of free citizens not large enough to make Property a general character of that society, while the rest are dispossessed of the means of production and are therefore proletarian, we call *Capitalist*."

Note the several points of such a state of affairs. You have private ownership; but it is not private ownership distributed in many hands and thus familiar as an institution to society as a whole. Again, you have the great majority dispossessed but at the same time citizens, that is, men politically free to act, though economically impotent; again, though it is but an inference from our definition, it is a necessary inference that there will be under Capitalism a conscious, direct, and planned *exploitation* of the majority (the free citizens who do not own) by the minority who are owners. For wealth must be produced: the whole of that community must live: and the possessors can make such terms with the non-possessors as shall make it certain that a portion of what the non-possessors have produced shall go to the possessors.

A society thus constituted cannot endure. It cannot endure because it is subject to two very severe strains: strains which increase in severity in proportion as that society becomes more thoroughly Capitalist. The first of these strains arises from the divergence between the moral theories upon which the State reposes and the social facts which those moral theories attempt to govern. The second strain arises from the insecurity to which Capitalism condemns the great mass of society, and the general character of anxiety and peril which it imposes upon all citizens, but in particular upon the majority, which consists, under Capitalism, of dispossessed free men.

Of these two strains it is impossible to say which is the gravest. Either would be enough to destroy a social arrangement in which it was long present. The two combined make that destruction certain; and there is no longer any doubt that Capitalist society must transform itself into some other and more stable arrangement. It is the object of these pages to discover what that stable arrangement will probably be.

We say that there is a moral strain already intolerably severe and growing more severe with every perfection of Capitalism.

This moral strain comes from a contradiction between the realities of Capitalist society and the moral base of our laws and traditions.

The moral base upon which our laws are still administered and our conventions raised presupposes a state composed of free citizens. Our law defends property as a normal institution with which all citizens are acquainted, and which all citizens respect. It punishes theft as an abnormal incident only occurring when, through evil motives, one free citizen acquires the property of another without his knowledge and against his will. It punishes fraud as another abnormal incident in which, from evil motives, one free citizen induces another to part with his property upon false representations. It enforces contract, the sole moral base of which is the freedom of the two contracting parties, and the power of either, if it so please him, not to enter into a contract which, once entered into, must be enforced. It gives to an owner the power to leave his property by will, under the conception that such ownership and such passage of property (to natural heirs as a rule, but exceptionally to any other whom the testator may point out) is the normal operation of a society generally familiar with such things, and finding them part of the domestic life lived by the mass of its citizens. It casts one citizen in damages if by any wilful action he has caused loss to another—for it presupposes him able to pay.

The sanction upon which social life reposes is, in our moral theory, the legal punishment enforceable in our Courts, and the basis presupposed for the security and material happiness of our citizens is the possession of goods which shall guarantee us from anxiety and permit us an independence of action in the midst of our fellowmen.

Now contrast all this, the moral theory upon which society is still perilously conducted, the moral theory to which Capitalism itself turns for succour when it is attacked, contrast, I say, its formulæ and its presuppositions with the social reality of a Capitalist State such as is England to-day.

Property remains as an instinct perhaps with most of the citizens; as an experience and a reality it is unknown to nineteen out of twenty. One hundred forms of fraud, the necessary corollary of unrestrained competition between a few and of unrestrained avarice as the motive controlling production, are not or cannot be punished: petty forms of violence in theft and of cunning in fraud the laws can deal with, but they can deal with these alone. Our legal machinery has become little more than an engine for protecting the few owners against the necessities, the demands, or the hatred of the mass of their dispossessed fellow-citizens. The vast bulk of so-called " free " contracts are to-day leonine contracts: arrangements which one man was free to take or to leave, but which the other man was not free to take or to leave, because the second had for his alternative starvation.

Most important of all, the fundamental social fact of our movement, far more important than any security afforded by law, or than any machinery which the State can put into action, is the fact that *livelihood* is at the will of the possessors. It can be granted by the possessors to the non-possessors, or it can be withheld. The real sanction in our society for the arrangements by which it is conducted is not punishment enforceable by the Courts, but the withholding of livelihood from the dispossessed by the possessors. Most men now fear the loss of employment more than they fear legal punishment, and the discipline under which men are coerced in their modern forms of activity in England is the fear of dismissal. The true master of the Englishman to-day is not the Sovereign nor the officers of State, nor, save indirectly, the laws; his true master is the Capitalist.

Of these main truths everyone is aware ; and anyone who sets out to deny them does so to-day at the peril of his reputation either for honesty or for intelligence.

If it be asked why things have come to a head so late (Capitalism having been in growth for so long), the answer is that England, even now the most completely Capitalist State of the modern world, did not itself become a completely Capitalist State until the present generation. Within the memory of men now living half England was agricultural, with relations domestic rather than competitive between the various human factors to production.

This moral strain, therefore, arising from the divergence between what our laws and moral phrases pretend, and what our society actually is, makes of that society an utterly unstable thing.

This spiritual thesis is of far greater gravity than the narrow materialism of a generation now passing might imagine. Spiritual conflict is more fruitful of instability in the State than conflict of any other kind, and there is acute spiritual conflict, conflict in every man's conscience and ill-ease throughout the commonwealth when the realities of society are divorced from the moral base of its institutions.

The second strain which we have noted in Capitalism, its second element of instability, consists in the fact that Capitalism destroys security.

STATE GROWS UNSTABLE

Experience is enough to save us any delay upon this main point of our matter. But even without experience we could reason with absolute certitude from the very nature of Capitalism that its chief effect would be the destruction of security in human life.

Combine these two elements: the ownership of the means of production by a very few; the political freedom of owners and non-owners alike. There follows immediately from that combination a competitive market wherein the labour of the non-owner fetches just what it is worth, not as full productive power, but as productive power which will leave a surplus to the Capitalist. It fetches nothing when the labourer cannot work, more in proportion to the pace at which he is driven; less in middle age than in youth; less in old age than in middle age; nothing in sickness; nothing in despair.

A man in a position to accumulate (the normal result of human labour), a man founded upon property in sufficient amount and in established form is no more productive in his non-productive moments than is a proletarian; but his life is balanced and regulated by his reception of rent and interest as well as wages. Surplus values come to him, and are the fly-wheel balancing the extremes of his life and carrying him over his bad times. With a proletarian it cannot be so. The aspect whence Capital looks at a human being whose labour it proposes to purchase cuts right across that normal aspect of human life from which we all regard our own affections, duties, and character. A man thinks of himself, of his chances and of his security along the line of his own individual existence from birth to death. Capital purchasing his labour (and not the man himself) purchases but a cross-section of his life, his moments of activity. For the rest, he must fend for himself; but to fend for yourself when you have nothing is to starve.

As a matter of fact, where a few possess the means of production perfectly free political conditions are impossible. A perfect Capitalist State cannot exist, though we have come nearer to it in modern England than other and more fortunate nations had thought possible. In the perfect Capitalist State there would be no food available for the non-owner save when he was actually engaged in Production, and that absurdity would, by quickly ending all human lives save those of the owners, put a term to the arrangement. If you left men completely free under a Capitalist system, there would be so heavy a mortality from starvation as would dry up the sources of labour in a very short time.

Imagine the dispossessed to be ideally perfect cowards, the possessors to consider nothing whatsoever except the buying of their labour in the cheapest market—and the system would break down from the death of children and of out-o'-works and of women. You would not have a State in mere decline such as ours is. You would have a State manifestly and patently perishing.

As a fact, of course, Capitalism cannot proceed to its own logical extreme. So long as the political freedom of all citizens is granted [the freedom of the few possessors of food to grant or withhold it, of the many non-possessors to strike any bargain at all, lest they lack it]: to exercise such freedom fully is to starve the very young, the old, the impotent, and the despairing to death. Capitalism must keep alive, by non-Capitalist methods, great masses of the population who would otherwise starve to death; and that is what Capitalism was careful to do to an increasing extent as it got a stronger and a stronger grip upon the English people. Elizabeth's Poor Law at the beginning of the business, the Poor Law of 1834, coming at a moment when nearly half England had passed into the grip of Capitalism, are original and primitive instances : there are to-day a hundred others.

Though this cause of insecurity—the fact that the possessors have no direct incentive to keep men alive —is logically the most obvious, and always the most enduring under a Capitalist system, there is another cause more poignant in its effect upon human life. That other cause is the competitive anarchy in production which restricted ownership coupled with freedom involves. Consider what is involved by the very process of production where the implements and the soil are in the hands of a few whose motive for causing the proletariat to produce is not the use of the wealth created but the enjoyment by those possessors of surplus value or " profit."

If full political freedom be allowed to any two such possessors of implements and stores, each will actively watch his market, attempt to undersell the other, tend to overproduce at the end of some season of extra demand for his article, thus glut the market only to suffer a period of depression afterwards—and so forth. Again, the Capitalist, free, individual director of production, will miscalculate ; sometimes he will fail, and his works will be shut down. Again, a mass of isolated, imperfectly instructed competing units cannot but direct their clashing efforts at an enormous waste, and that waste will fluctuate. Most commissions, most advertisements, most parades, are examples of this waste. If this waste of effort could be made a constant, the parasitical employment it afforded would be a constant too. But of its nature it is a most inconstant thing, and the employment it affords is therefore necessarily precarious. The concrete translation of this is the insecurity of the commercial traveller, the advertising agent, the insurance agent, and every form of touting and cozening which competitive Capitalism carries with it.

Now here again, as in the case of the insecurity produced by age and sickness, Capitalism cannot be pursued to its logical conclusion, and it is the element of freedom which suffers. Competition is, as a fact, restricted to an increasing extent by an understanding between the competitors, accompanied, especially in this country, by the ruin of the smaller competitor through secret conspiracies entered into by the larger men, and supported by the secret political forces of the State.* In a word, Capitalism, proving almost as unstable to the owners as to the non-owners, is tending towards stability by losing its essential character of political freedom. No better proof of the instability of Capitalism as a system could be desired.

Take any one of the numerous Trusts which now control English industry, and have made of modern England the type, quoted throughout the Continent, of artificial monopolies. If the full formula of Capitalism were accepted by our Courts and our executive statesmen, anyone could start a rival business, undersell those Trusts and shatter the comparative security they afford to industry within their field. The reason that no one does this is that political free-

---

* Before any trust is established in this country, the first step is to "interest" one of our politicians. The Telephones, the South Wales Coal Trust, the happily defeated Soap Trust, the Soda, Fish, and Fruit Trusts, are examples in point.

dom is not, as a fact, protected here by the Courts in commercial affairs. A man attempting to compete with one of our great English Trusts would find himself at once undersold. He might, by all the spirit of European law for centuries, indict those who would ruin him, citing them for a conspiracy in restraint of trade; of this conspiracy he would find the judge and the politicians most heartily in support.

But it must always be remembered that these conspiracies in restraint of trade which are the mark of modern England are in themselves a mark of the transition from the true Capitalist phase to another.

Under the essential conditions of Capitalism— under a perfect political freedom—such conspiracies would be punished by the Courts for what they are: to wit, a contravention of the fundamental doctrine of political liberty. For this doctrine, while it gives any man the right to make any contract he chooses with any labourer and offer the produce at such prices as he sees fit, also involves the protection of that liberty by the punishment of any conspiracy that may have monopoly for its object. If such perfect freedom is no longer attempted, if monopolies are permitted and fostered, it is because the unnatural strain to which freedom, coupled with restricted ownership, gives rise, the insecurity of its mere competition, the anarchy of its productive methods have at last proved intolerable.

STATE GROWS UNSTABLE

I have already delayed more than was necessary in this section upon the causes which render a Capitalist State essentially unstable.

I might have treated the matter empirically, taking for granted the observation which all my readers must have made, that Capitalism is as a fact doomed, and that the Capitalist State has already passed into its first phase of transition.

We are clearly no longer possessed of that absolute political freedom which true Capitalism essentially demands. The insecurity involved, coupled with the divorce between our traditional morals and the facts of society, have already introduced such novel features as the permission of conspiracy among both possessors and non-possessors, the compulsory provision of security through State action, and all these reforms, implicit or explicit, the tendency of which I am about to examine.

THE STABLE SOLUTIONS OF THIS INSTABILITY

SECTION THE SIXTH   THE STABLE SOLUTIONS OF THIS INSTABILITY

GIVEN A CAPITALIST STATE, OF ITS nature unstable, it will tend to reach stability by some method or another.

It is the definition of unstable equilibrium that a body in unstable equilibrium is seeking a stable equilibrium. For instance, a pyramid balanced upon its apex is in unstable equilibrium; which simply means that a slight force one way or the other will make it fall into a position where it will repose. Similarly, certain chemical mixtures are said to be in unstable equilibrium when their constituent parts have such affinity one for another that a slight shock may make them combine and transform the chemical arrangement of the whole. Of this sort are explosives.

If the Capitalist State is in unstable equilibrium, this only means that it is seeking a stable equilibrium, and that Capitalism cannot but be transformed into some other arrangement wherein Society may repose.

There are but three social arrangements which can replace Capitalism: Slavery, Socialism, and Property.

I may imagine a mixture of any two of these three or of all the three, but each is a dominant type, and from the very nature of the problem no fourth arrangement can be devised.

The problem turns, remember, upon the control of the means of production. Capitalism means that this control is vested in the hands of few, while political freedom is the appanage of all. If this anomaly cannot endure, from its insecurity and from its own contradiction with its presumed moral basis, you must either have a transformation of the one or of the other of the two elements which combined have been found unworkable. These two factors are (1) The ownership of the means of Production by a few; (2) The Freedom of all. To solve Capitalism you must get rid of restricted ownership, or of freedom, or of both.

Now there is only one alternative to freedom, which is the negation of it. Either a man is free to work and not to work as he pleases, or he may be liable to a legal compulsion to work, backed by the forces of the State. In the first he is a free man; in the second he is by definition a slave. We have, therefore, so far as this factor of freedom is concerned, no choice between a number of changes, but only the opportunity of one, to wit, the establishment of slavery in place of freedom. Such a solution, the direct, immediate, and conscious re-establishment of slavery, would provide a true solution of the problems which Capitalism offers. It would guarantee, under workable regulations, sufficiency and security for the dispossessed. Such a solution, as I shall show, is the probable goal which our society will in fact approach To its immediate and conscious acceptance, however, there is an obstacle.

A direct and conscious establishment of slavery as a solution to the problem of Capitalism, the surviving Christian tradition of our civilisation compels men to reject. No reformer will advocate it; no prophet dares take it as yet for granted. All theories of a reformed society will therefore attempt, at first, to leave untouched the factor of *Freedom* among the elements which make up Capitalism, and will concern themselves with some change in the factor of *Property*.*

Now, in attempting to remedy the evils of Capitalism by remedying that one of its two factors which consists in an ill distribution of property, you have two, and only two, courses open to you.

If you are suffering because property is restricted to a few, you can alter that factor in the problem *either* by putting property into the hands of many, *or* by putting it into the hands of none. There is no third course.

In the concrete, to put property in the hands of none" means to vest it as a trust in the hands of political officers. If you say that the evils proceeding from Capitalism are due to the institution of property itself, and not to the dispossession of the many by the few, then you must forbid the private possession of the means of production by any particular and

* By which word "*property*" is meant, of course, property in the means of Production.

private part of the community: but someone must control the means of production, or we should have nothing to eat. So in practice this doctrine means the management of the means of production by those who are the public officers of the community. Whether these public officers are themselves controlled by the community or no has nothing to do with this solution on its economic side. The essential point to grasp is that the only alternative to private property is public property. Somebody must see to the ploughing and must control the ploughs; otherwise no ploughing will be done.

It is equally obvious that if you conclude property in itself to be no evil but only the small number of its owners, then your remedy is to increase the number of those owners.

So much being grasped, we may recapitulate and say that a society like ours, disliking the name of "slavery," and avoiding a direct and conscious re-establishment of the slave status, will necessarily contemplate the reform of its ill-distributed ownership on one of two models. The first is the negation of private property and the establishment of what is called Collectivism: that is, the management of the means of production by the political officers of the community. The second is the wider distribution of property until that institution shall become the mark of the whole State, and until free citizens are nornally found to be possessors of capital or land, or both.

The first model we call *Socialism* or the Collectivist State; the second we call the Proprietary or Distributive State.

With so much elucidated, I will proceed to show in my next section why the second model, involving the redistribution of property, is rejected as impracticable by our existing Capitalist Society, and why, therefore, the model chosen by reformers is the first model, that of a Collectivist State.

I shall then proceed to show that at its first inception all Collectivist Reform is necessarily deflected and evolves, in the place of what it had intended, a new thing: a society wherein the owners remain few and wherein the proletarian mass accepts security at the expense of servitude.

Have I made myself clear?

If not, I will repeat for the third time, and in its briefest terms, the formula which is the kernel of my whole thesis.

The Capitalist State breeds a Collectivist Theory which *in action* produces something utterly different from Collectivism: to wit, the SERVILE STATE.

SOCIALISM IS THE EASIEST APPARENT SOLUTION OF THE CAPITALIST CRUX

I SAY THAT THE LINE OF LEAST RESIST-
ance, if it be followed, leads a Capitalist State to transform itself into a Servile State.

I propose to show that this comes about from the
fact that not a *Distributive* but a *Collectivist* solution
is the easiest for a Capitalist State to aim at, and that
yet, in the very act of attempting *Collectivism*, what
results is not Collectivism at all, but the servitude of
the many, and the confirmation in their present privilege of the few ; that is, the Servile State.

Men to whom the institution of slavery is abhorrent propose for the remedy of Capitalism one of
two reforms.

Either they would put property into the hands of
most citizens, so dividing land and capital that a determining number of families in the State were possessed of the means of production ; or they would put
those means of production into the hands of the political officers of the community, to be held in trust
for the advantage of all.

The first solution may be called the attempted
establishment of the DISTRIBUTIVE STATE. The
second may be called the attempted establishment
of the COLLECTIVIST STATE.

Those who favour the first course are the Conservatives or Traditionalists. They are men who respect and would, if possible, preserve the old forms of Christian European life. They know that property was thus distributed throughout the State during the happiest periods of our past history; they also know that where it is properly distributed to-day, you have greater social sanity and ease than elsewhere. In general, those who would re-establish, if possible, the Distributive State in the place of, and as a remedy for, the vices and unrest of Capitalism, are men concerned with known realities, and having for their goal a condition of society which experience has tested and proved both stable and good. They are then of the two schools of reformers, the more *practical* in the sense that they deal more than do the Collectivists (called also Socialists) with things which either are or have been in actual existence. But they are less practical in another sense (as we shall see in a moment) from the fact that the stage of the disease with which they are dealing does not readily lend itself to such a reaction as they propose.

The Collectivist, on the other hand, proposes to put land and capital into the hands of the political officer of the community, and this on the understanding that they shall hold such land and capital in trust for the advantage of the community. In making this proposal he is evidently dealing with a state of things hitherto imaginary, and his ideal is not one that ha been tested by experience, nor one of which our race and history can furnish instances. In this sense, therefore, he is the *less* practical of the two reformers. His ideal cannot be discovered in any past, known, and recorded phase of our society. We cannot examine Socialism in actual working, nor can we say (as we can say of well-divided property): "On such and such an occasion, in such and such a period of European history, Collectivism was established and produced both stability and happiness in society."

In this sense, therefore, the Collectivist is far less practical than the reformer who desires well-distributed property.

On the other hand, there is a sense in which this Socialist is more practical than that other type of reformer, from the fact that the stage of the disease into which we have fallen apparently admits of his remedy with less shock than it admits of a reaction towards well-divided property.

For example: the operation of buying out some great tract of private ownership to-day (as a railway or a harbour company) with public funds, continuing its administration by publicly paid officials and converting its revenue to public use, is a thing with which we are familiar and which seemingly might be indefinitely multiplied. Individual examples of such transformation of waterworks, gas, tramways, from a Capitalist to a Collectivist basis are common, and the change does not disturb any fundamental thing in our society. When a private Water company or Tramway line is bought by some town and worked thereafter in the interests of the public, the transaction is effected without any perceptible friction, disturbs the life of no private citizen, and seems in every way normal to the society in which it takes place.

Upon the contrary, the attempt to create a large number of shareholders in such enterprises and artificially to substitute many partners, distributed throughout a great number of the population, in the place of the original few capitalist owners, would prove lengthy and at every step would arouse opposition, would create disturbance, would work at an expense of great friction, and would be imperilled by the power of the new and many owners to sell again to a few.

In a word, the man who desires to re-establish property as an institution normal to most citizens in the State is *working against the grain* of our existing Capitalist society, while a man who desires to establish Socialism—that is Collectivism—is working *with* the grain of that society. The first is like a physician who should say to a man whose limbs were partially atrophied from disuse: " Do this and that, take such and such exercise, and you will recover the use of your limbs." The second is like a physician who should say : " You cannot go on as you are. Your limbs are atrophied from lack of use. Your attempt to conduct yourself as though they were not is useless and painful ; you had better make up your mind to be wheeled about in a fashion consonant to your disease." The Physician is the Reformer, his Patient the Proletariat.

It is not the purpose of this book to show how and under what difficulties a condition of well-divided property might be restored and might take the place (even in England) of that Capitalism which is now no longer either stable or tolerable ; but for the purposes of contrast and to emphasise my argument I will proceed, before showing how the Collectivist unconsciously makes for the Servile State, to show what difficulties surround the Distributive solution and why, therefore, the Collectivist solution appeals so much more readily to men living under Capitalism.

If I desire to substitute a number of small owners for a few large ones in some particular enterprise, how shall I set to work?

I might boldly confiscate and redistribute at a blow. But by what process should I choose the new owners? Even supposing that there was some machinery whereby the justice of the new distribution could be assured, how could I avoid the enormous and innumerable separate acts of injustice that would attach to general redistributions? To say "none shall own" and to confiscate is one thing; to say "all should

109

own" and apportion ownership is another. Action of this kind would so disturb the whole network of economic relations as to bring ruin at once to the whole body politic, and particularly to the smaller interests indirectly affected. In a society such as ours a catastrophe falling upon the State from outside might indirectly do good by making such a redistribution possible. But no one working from within the State could provoke that catastrophe without ruining his own cause.

If, then, I proceed more slowly and more rationally and canalise the economic life of society so that small property shall gradually be built up within it, see against what forces of inertia and custom I have to work to-day in a Capitalist society!

If I desire to benefit small savings at the expense of large, I must reverse the whole economy under which interest is paid upon deposits to-day. It is far easier to save £100 out of a revenue of £1000 than to save £10 out of a revenue of £100. It is infinitely easier to save £10 out of a revenue of £100 than £5 out of a revenue of £50. To build up small property through thrift when once the Mass have fallen into the proletarian trough is impossible unless you deliberately subsidise small savings, offering them a reward which, in competition, they could never obtain; and to do this the whole vast arrangement of credit must be worked backwards. Or, let the policy be pursued of penalising undertakings with few owners, of heavily taxing large blocks of shares and of subsidising with the produce small holders in proportion to the small-ness of their holding. Here again you are met with the difficulty of a vast majority who cannot even bid for the smallest share.

One might multiply instances of the sort indefi-nitely, but the strongest force against the distribution of ownership in a society already permeated with Capitalist modes of thought is still the moral one: Will men want to own? Will officials, administrators, and law-makers be able to shake off the power which under Capitalism seems normal to the rich? If I ap-proach, for instance, the works of one of our great Trusts, purchase it with public money, bestow, even as a gift, the shares thereof to its workmen; can I count upon any tradition of property in their midst which will prevent their squandering the new wealth? Can I discover any relics of the co-operative instinct among such men? Could I get managers and organisers to take a group of poor men seriously or to serve them as they would serve rich men? Is not the whole psy-chology of a Capitalist society divided between the proletarian mass which thinks in terms not of pro-perty but of "employment," and the few owners who are alone familiar with the machinery of administra-tion?

I have touched but very briefly and superficially

upon this matter, because it needs no elaboration. Though it is evident that with a sufficient will and a sufficient social vitality property could be restored, it is evident that all efforts to restore it have in a Capitalist society such as our own a note of oddity, of doubtful experiment, of being unco-ordinated with other social things around them, which marks the heavy handicap under which any such attempt must proceed. It is like recommending elasticity to the aged.

On the other hand, the Collectivist experiment is thoroughly suited (in appearance at least) to the Capitalist society which it proposes to replace. It works with the existing machinery of Capitalism, talks and thinks in the existing terms of Capitalism, appeals to just those appetites which Capitalism has aroused, and ridicules as fantastic and unheard-of just those things in society the memory of which Capitalism has killed among men wherever the blight of it has spread.

So true is all this that the stupider kind of Collectivist will often talk of a "Capitalist phase" of society as the necessary precedent to a "Collectivist phase." A trust or monopoly is welcomed because it "furnishes a mode of transition from private to public ownership." Collectivism promises employment to the great mass who think of production only in terms of employment. It promises to its workmen the security which a great and well-organised industrial Capitalist unit (like one of our railways) can give through a system of pensions, regular promotion, etc., but that security vastly increased through the fact that it is the State and not a mere unit of the State which guarantees it. Collectivism would administer, would pay wages, would promote, would pension off, would fine—and all the rest of it—exactly as the Capitalist State does to-day. The proletarian, when the Collectivist (or Socialist) State is put before him, perceives nothing in the picture save certain ameliorations of his present position. Who can imagine that if, say, two of our great industries, Coal and Railways, were handed over to the State to-morrow, the armies of men organised therein would find any change in the character of their lives, save in some increase of security and possibly in a very slight increase of earnings?

The whole scheme of Collectivism presents, so far as the proletarian mass of a Capitalist State is concerned, nothing unknown at all, but a promise of some increment in wages and a certainty of far greater ease of mind.

To that small minority of a Capitalist society which owns the means of production, Collectivism will of course appear as an enemy, but, even so, it is an enemy which they understand and an enemy with whom they can treat in terms common both to that enemy and to themselves. If, for instance, the State proposes to take over such and such a trust now paying 4 per cent., and believes that under State management it will make the trust pay 5 per cent., then the transference takes the form of a business proposition: the State is no harder to the Capitalists taken over than was Mr Yerkes to the Underground. Again, the State, having greater credit and longevity, can (it would seem)* "buy out" any existing Capitalist body upon favourable terms. Again, the discipline by which the State would enforce its rules upon the proletariat it employed would be the same rules as those by which the Capitalist imposes discipline in his own interests to-day.

There is in the whole scheme which proposes to transform the Capitalist into the Collectivist State no element of reaction, the use of no term with which a Capitalist society is not familiar, the appeal to no instinct, whether of cowardice, greed, apathy, or mechanical regulation, with which a Capitalist community is not amply familiar.

In general, if modern Capitalist England were made by magic a State of small owners, we should all suffer an enormous revolution. We should marvel at the insolence of the poor, at the laziness of the contented, at the strange diversities of task, at the rebellious,

* That this is an illusion I shall attempt to show on a later page.

vigorous personalities discernible upon every side. But if this modern Capitalist England could, by a process sufficiently slow to allow for the readjustment of individual interests, be transformed into a Collectivist State, the apparent change at the end of that transition would not be conspicuous to the most of us, and the transition itself should have met with no shocks that theory can discover. The insecure and hopeless margin below the regularly paid ranks of labour would have disappeared into isolated workplaces of a penal kind: we should hardly miss them. Many incomes now involving considerable duties to the State would have been replaced by incomes as large or larger, involving much the same duties and bearing only the newer name of salaries. The small shop-keeping class would find itself in part absorbed under public schemes at a salary, in part engaged in the old work of distribution at secure incomes; and such small owners as were left, of boats, of farms, even of machinery, would perhaps know the new state of things into which they had survived through nothing more novel than some increase in the irritating system of inspection and of onerous petty taxation: they are already fairly used to both.

This picture of the natural transition from Capitalism to Collectivism seems so obvious that many Collectivists in a generation immediately past believed that nothing stood between them and the realisation of their ideal save the unintelligence of mankind. They had only to argue and expound patiently and systematically for the great transformation to become possible. They had only to continue arguing and expounding for it at last to be realised.

I say, "of the last generation." To-day that simple and superficial judgment is getting woefully disturbed. The most sincere and single-minded of Collectivists cannot but note that the practical effect of their propaganda is not an approach towards the Collectivist State at all, but towards something very different. It is becoming more and more evident that with every new reform—and those reforms commonly promoted by particular Socialists, and in a puzzled way blessed by Socialists in general—another state emerges more and more clearly. It is becoming increasingly certain that the attempted transformation of Capitalism into Collectivism is resulting not in Collectivism at all, but in some third thing which the Collectivist never dreamt of, or the Capitalist either; and that third thing is the SERVILE State : a State, that is, in which the mass of men shall be constrained *by law* to labour to the profit of a minority, but, as the price of such constraint, shall enjoy a security which the old Capitalism did not give them.

Why is the apparently simple and direct action of Collectivist reform diverted into so unexpected a channel? And in what new laws and institutions does

EASIEST SOLUTION

modern England in particular and industrial society
in general show that this new form of the State is
upon us?

To these two questions I will attempt an answer in
the two concluding divisions of this book.

THE REFORMERS AND THE REFORMED ARE ALIKE MAKING FOR THE SERVILE STATE

SECTION EIGHT   THE REFORMERS AND THE REFORMED ARE ALIKE MAKING FOR THE SERVILE STATE

I PROPOSE IN THIS SECTION TO SHOW how the three interests which between them account for nearly the whole of the forces making for social change in modern England are all necessarily drifting towards the Servile State.

Of these three interests the first two represent the Reformers—the third the people to be Reformed.

These three interests are, first, the *Socialist*, who is the theoretical reformer working along the line of least resistance; secondly, the "*Practical Man*," who as a "practical" reformer depends on his shortness of sight, and is therefore to-day a powerful factor; while the third is that great proletarian mass for whom the change is being effected, and on whom it is being imposed. What *they* are most likely to accept, the way in which *they* will react upon new institutions is the most important factor of all, for they are the material with and upon which the work is being done.

(1) Of the *Socialist* Reformer :

I say that men attempting to achieve Collectivism or Socialism as the remedy for the evils of the Capitalist State find themselves drifting not towards a Collectivist State at all, but towards a Servile State.

The Socialist movement, the first of the three factors in this drift, is itself made up of two kinds

THE SERVILE STATE

of men: there is (*a*) the man who regards the public ownership of the means of production (and the consequent compulsion of all citizens to work under the direction of the State) as the only feasible solution of our modern social ills. There is also (*b*) the man who loves the Collectivist ideal in itself, who does not pursue it so much because it is a solution of modern Capitalism, as because it is an ordered and regular form of society which appeals to him in itself. He loves to consider the ideal of a State in which land and capital shall be held by public officials who shall order other men about and so preserve them from the consequences of *their* vice, ignorance, and folly.

These types are perfectly distinct, in many respects antagonistic, and between them they cover the whole Socialist movement.

Now imagine either of these men at issue with the existing state of Capitalist society and attempting to transform it. Along what line of least resistance will either be led?

(*a*) The first type will begin by demanding the confiscation of the means of production from the hands of their present owners, and the vesting of them in the State. But wait a moment. That demand is an exceedingly hard thing to accomplish. The present owners have between them and confiscation a stony moral barrier. It is what *most* men would call the moral basis of property (the instinct that property is a *right*), and what *all* men would admit to be at least a deeply rooted tradition. Again, they have behind them the innumerable complexities of modern ownership.

To take a very simple case. Decree that all common lands enclosed since so late a date as 1760 shall revert to the public. There you have a very moderate case and a very defensible one. But conceive for a moment how many small freeholds, what a nexus of obligation and benefit spread over millions, what thousands of exchanges, what purchases made upon the difficult savings of small men such a measure would wreck! It is conceivable, for, in the moral sphere, society can do anything to society; but it would bring crashing down with it twenty times the wealth involved and all the secure credit of our community. In a word, the thing is, in the conversational use of that term, impossible. So your best type of Socialist reformer is led to an expedient which I will here only mention—as it must be separately considered at length later on account of its fundamental importance—the expedient of "*buying out*" the present owner.

It is enough to say in this place that the attempt to "buy out" without confiscation is based upon an economic error. This I shall prove in its proper place. For the moment I assume it and pass on to the rest of my reformer's action.

123

He does not confiscate, then; at the most he "buys out" (or attempts to "buy out") certain sections of the means of production.

But this action by no means covers the whole of his motive. By definition the man is out to cure what he sees to be the great immediate evils of Capitalist society. He is out to cure the destitution which it causes in great multitudes and the harrowing insecurity which it imposes upon all. He is out to substitute for Capitalist society a society in which men shall all be fed, clothed, housed, and in which men shall not live in a perpetual jeopardy of their housing, clothing, and food.

Well, there is a way of achieving that without confiscation.

This reformer rightly thinks that the ownership of the means of production by a few has caused the evils which arouse his indignation and pity. But they have only been so caused on account of a combination of such limited ownership with universal freedom. The combination of the two is the very definition of the Capitalist State. It is difficult indeed to dispossess the possessors. It is by no means so difficult (as we shall see again when we are dealing with the mass whom these changes will principally affect) to modify the factor of freedom.

You can say to the Capitalist: "I desire to dispossess you, and meanwhile I am determined that your employees shall live tolerable lives." The Capitalist replies : " I refuse to be dispossessed, and it is, short of catastrophe, impossible to dispossess me. But if you will define the relation between my employees and myself, I will undertake particular responsibilities due to my position. Subject the proletarian, as a proletarian, and because he is a proletarian, to special laws. Clothe me, the Capitalist, as a Capitalist, and because I am a Capitalist, with special converse duties under those laws. I will faithfully see that they are obeyed; I will compel my employees to obey them, and I will undertake the new rôle imposed upon me by the State. Nay, I will go further, and I will say that such a novel arrangement will make my own profits perhaps larger and certainly more secure."

This idealist social reformer, therefore, finds the current of his demand canalised. As to one part of it, confiscation, it is checked and barred; as to the other, securing human conditions for the proletariat, the gates are open. Half the river is dammed by a strong weir, but there is a sluice, and that sluice can be lifted. Once lifted, the whole force of the current will run through the opportunity so afforded it; there will it scour and deepen its channel; there will the main stream learn to run.

To drop the metaphor, all those things in the true

Socialist's demand which are compatible with the Servile State can certainly be achieved. The first steps towards them are already achieved. They are of such a nature that upon them can be based a further advance in the same direction, and the whole Capitalist State can be rapidly and easily transformed into the Servile State, satisfying in its transformation the more immediate claims and the more urgent demands of the social reformer whose ultimate objective indeed may be the public ownership of capital and land, but whose driving power is a burning pity for the poverty and peril of the masses.

When the transformation is complete there will be no ground left, nor any demand or necessity, for public ownership. The reformer only asked for it in order to secure security and sufficiency: he has obtained his demand.

Here are security and sufficiency achieved by another and much easier method, consonant with and proceeding from the Capitalist phase immediately preceding it: there is no need to go further.

In this way the Socialist whose motive is human good and not mere organisation is being shepherded in spite of himself *away* from his Collectivist ideal and *towards* a society in which the possessors shall remain possessed, the dispossessed shall remain dispossessed, in which the mass of men shall still work for the advantage of a few, and in which those few shall still enjoy the surplus values produced by labour, but in which the special evils of insecurity and insufficiency, in the main the product of freedom, have been eliminated by the destruction of freedom.

At the end of the process you will have two kinds of men, the owners economically free, and controlling to their peace and to the guarantee of their livelihood the economically unfree non-owners. But that is the Servile State.

(*b*) The second type of socialist reformer may be dealt with more briefly. In him the exploitation of man by man excites no indignation. Indeed, he is not of a type to which indignation or any other lively passion is familiar. Tables, statistics, an exact framework for life—these afford him the food that satisfies his moral apetite; the occupation most congenial to him is the "running" of men: as a machine is run.

To such a man the Collectivist ideal particularly appeals.

It is orderly in the extreme. All that human and organic complexity which is the colour of any vital society offends him by its infinite differentiation. He is disturbed by multitudinous things; and the prospect of a vast bureaucracy wherein the whole of life shall be scheduled and appointed to certain simple schemes deriving from the co-ordinate work of public clerks and marshalled by powerful heads of departments

127

gives his small stomach a final satisfaction.

Now this man, like the other, would prefer to begin with public property in capital and land, and upon that basis to erect the formal scheme which so suits his peculiar temperament. (It nee   hardly be said that in his vision of a future society he conceives of himself as the head of at least a department and possibly of the whole State—but that is by the way.) But while he would prefer to begin with a Collectivist scheme ready-made, he finds in practice that he cannot do so. He would have to confiscate, just as the more hearty Socialist would; and if that act is very difficult to the man burning at the sight of human wrongs, how much more difficult is it to a man impelled by no such motive force and directed by nothing more intense than a mechanical appetite for regulation?

He cannot confiscate or begin to confiscate. At the best he will "buy out" the Capitalist.

Now, in his case, as in the case of the more human Socialist, "buying out" is, as I shall show in its proper place, a system impossible of general application.

But all those other things for which such a man cares much more than he does for the socialisation of the means of production—tabulation, detailed administration of men, the co-ordination of many efforts under one schedule, the elimination of all private power to react against his Department, all these are immediately obtainable without disturbing the existing arrangement of society. With him, precisely as with the other socialist, what he desires can be reached without any dispossession of the few existing possessors. He has but to secure the registration of the proletariat; next to ensure that neither they in the exercise of their freedom, nor the employer in the exercise of his, can produce insufficiency or insecurity—and he is content. Let laws exist which make the proper housing, feeding, clothing, and recreation of the proletarian mass be incumbent upon the possessing class, and the observance of such rules be imposed, by inspection and punishment, upon those whom he pretends to benefit, and all that he really cares for will be achieved.

To such a man the Servile State is hardly a thing towards which he drifts, it is rather a tolerable alternative to his ideal Collectivist State, which alternative he is quite prepared to accept and regards favourably. Already the greater part of such reformers who, a generation ago, would have called themselves "Socialists" are now less concerned with any scheme for socialising Capital and Land than with innumerable schemes actually existing, some of them possessing already the force of laws, for regulating, "running," and drilling the protelariat without trenching by an inch upon the privilege in implements, stores, and land enjoyed by the small Capitalist class.

The so-called "Socialist" of this type has not fallen into the Servile State by a miscalculation. He has fathered it; he welcomes its birth, he foresees his power over its future.

So much for the Socialist movement, which a generation ago proposed to transform our Capitalist society into one where the community should be the universal owner and all men equally economically free or unfree under its tutelage. To-day their ideal has failed, and of the two sources whence their energy proceeded, the one is reluctantly, the other gladly, acquiescent in the advent of a society which is not Socialist at all but Servile.

(2) Of the *Practical* Reformer:

There is another type of Reformer, one who prides himself on *not* being a socialist, and one of the greatest weight to-day. He also is making for the Servile State. This second factor in the change is the "Practical Man"; and this fool, on account of his great numbers and determining influence in the details of legislation, must be carefully examined.

It is your "Practical Man" who says: "Whatever you theorists and doctrinaires may hold with regard to this proposal (which I support), though it may offend some abstract dogma of yours, yet *in practice* you must admit that it does good. If you had *practical* experience of the misery of the Jones' family, or had done

130

practical work yourself in Pudsey, you would have seen that a *practical* man," etc.

It is not difficult to discern that the Practical Man in social reform is exactly the same animal as the Practical Man in every other department of human energy, and may be discovered suffering from the same twin disabilities which stamp the Practical Man wherever found: these twin disabilities are an inability to define his own first principles and an inability to follow the consequences proceeding from his own action. Both these disabilities proceed from one simple and deplorable form of impotence, the inability to think.

Let us help the Practical Man in his weakness and do a little thinking for him.

As a social reformer he has of course (though he does not know it) first principles and dogmas like all the rest of us, and *his* first principles and dogmas are exactly the same as those which his intellectual superiors hold in the matter of social reform. The two things intolerable to him as a decent citizen (though a very stupid human being) are *insufficiency* and *insecurity*. When he was "working" in the slums of Pudsey or raiding the proletarian Jones's from the secure base of Toynbee Hall, what shocked the worthy man most was "unemployment" and "destitution": that is, insecurity and insufficiency in flesh and blood.

Now, if the Socialist who has thought out his case, whether as a mere organiser or as a man hungering and thirsting after justice, is led away from Socialism and towards the Servile State by the force of modern things in England, how much more easily do you not think the "Practical Man" will be conducted towards that same Servile State, like any donkey to his grazing ground? To those dull and short-sighted eyes the immediate solution which even the beginnings of the Servile State propose are what a declivity is to a piece of brainless matter. The piece of brainless matter rolls down the declivity, and the Practical Man lollops from Capitalism to the Servile State with the same inevitable ease. Jones has not got enough. If you give him something in charity, that something will be soon consumed, and then Jones will again not have enough. Jones has been seven weeks out of work. If you get him work "under our unorganised and wasteful system, etc.," he may lose it just as he lost his first jobs. The slums of Pudsey, as the Practical Man knows by Practical experience, are often unemployable. Then there are "the ravages of drink": more fatal still the dreadful habit mankind has of forming families and breeding children. The worthy fellow notes that "as a practical matter of fact such men do not work unless you make them."

He does not, because he cannot, co-ordinate all these things. He knows nothing of a society in which free men were once owners, nor of the co-operative and instinctive institutions for the protection of ownership which such a society spontaneously breeds. He "takes the world as he finds it"—and the consequence is that whereas men of greater capacity may admit with different degrees of reluctance the general principles of the Servile State, *he*, the Practical Man, positively gloats on every new detail in the building up of that form of society. And the destruction of freedom by inches (though he does not see it to be the destruction of freedom) is the one panacea so obvious that he marvels at the doctrinaires who resist or suspect the process.

It has been necessary to waste so much time on this deplorable individual because the circumstances of our generation give him a peculiar power. Under the conditions of modern exchange a man of that sort enjoys great advantages. He is to be found as he never was in any other society before our own, possessed of wealth, and political as never was any such citizen until our time. Of history with all its lessons ; of the great schemes of philosophy and religion, of human nature itself he is blank.

The Practical Man left to himself would not produce the Servile State. He would not produce anything but a welter of anarchic restrictions which would lead at last to some kind of revolt.

Unfortunately, he is not left to himself. He is but the ally or flanking party of great forces which he does nothing to oppose, and of particular men, able

133

and prepared for the work of general change, who use him with gratitude and contempt. Were he not so numerous in modern England, and, under the extraordinary conditions of a Capitalist State, so economically powerful, I would have neglected him in this analysis. As it is, we may console ourselves by remembering that the advent of the Servile State, with its powerful organisation and necessity for lucid thought in those who govern, will certainly eliminate him.

Our reformers, then, both those who think and those who do not, both those who are conscious of the process and those who are unconscious of it, are making directly for the Servile State.

(3) What of the third factor? What of the people about to be reformed? What of the millions upon whose carcasses the reformers are at work, and who are the subject of the great experiment? Do they tend, as material, to accept or to reject that transformation from free proletarianism to servitude which is the argument of this book?

The question is an important one to decide, for upon whether the material is suitable or unsuitable for the work to which it is subjected, depends the success of every experiment making for the Servile State.

MAKING FOR SERVILE STATE

The mass of men in the Capitalist State is proletarian. As a matter of definition, the actual number of the proletariat and the proportion that number bears to the total number of families in the State may vary, but must be sufficient to determine the general character of the State before we can call that State *Capitalist*.

But, as we have seen, the Capitalist State is not a stable, and therefore not a permanent, condition of society. It has proved ephemeral; and upon that very account the proletariat in any Capitalist State retains to a greater or less degree some memories of a state of society in which its ancestors were possessors of property and economically free.

The strength of this memory or tradition is the first element we have to bear in mind in our problem, when we examine how far a particular proletariat, such as the English proletariat to-day, is ready to accept the Servile State which would condemn it to a perpetual loss of property and of all the free habit which property engenders.

Next be it noted that under conditions of freedom the Capitalist class may be entered by the more cunning or the more fortunate of the proletariat class. Recruitment of the kind was originally sufficiently common in the first development of Capitalism to be a standing feature in society and to impress the imagination of the general. Such recruitment is still possible. The proportion which it bears to the whole proletariat, the chance which each member of the proletariat may think he has of escaping from his proletarian condition in a particular phase of Capitalism such as is ours to-day, is the second factor in the problem.

The third factor, and by far the greatest of all, is the appetite of the dispossessed for that security and sufficiency of which Capitalism, with its essential condition of freedom, has deprived them.

Now let us consider the interplay of these three factors in the English proletariat as we actually know it at this moment. That proletariat is certainly the great mass of the State: it covers about nineteen-twentieths of the population—if we exclude Ireland, where, as I shall point out in my concluding pages, the reaction against Capitalism, and therefore against its development towards a Servile State, is already successful.

As to the first factor, it has changed very rapidly within the memory of men now living. The traditional rights of property are still strong in the minds of the English poor. All the moral connotations of that right are familiar to them. They are familiar with the conception of theft as a wrong; they are tenacious of any scraps of property which they may acquire. They could all explain what is meant by ownership, by legacy, by exchange, and by gift, and even by contract. There is not one but could put himself in the position, mentally, of an owner.

But the actual experience of ownership, and the effect which that experience has upon character and upon one's view of the State is a very different matter. Within the memory of people still living a sufficient number of Englishmen were owning (as small free-holders, small masters, etc.) to give to the institution of property coupled with freedom a very vivid effect upon the popular mind. More than this, there was a living tradition proceeding from the lips of men who could still bear living testimony to the relics of a better state of things. I have myself spoken, when I was a boy, to old labourers in the neighbourhood of Oxford who had risked their skins in armed protest against the enclosure of certain commons, and who had of course suffered imprisonment by a wealthy judge as the reward of their courage; and I have myself spoken in Lancashire to old men who could retrace for me, either from their personal experience the last phases of small ownership in the textile trade, or, from what their fathers had told them, the conditions of a time when small and well-divided ownership in cottage looms was actually common.

All that has passed. The last chapter of its passage has been singularly rapid. Roughly speaking, it is the generation brought up under the Education Acts of the last forty years which has grown up definitely and hopelessly proletarian. The present instinct, use, and meaning of property is lost to it: and this has had two very powerful effects, each strongly inclining our modern wage-earners to ignore the old barriers which lay between a condition of servitude and a condition of freedom. The first effect is this: that property is no longer what they seek, nor what they think obtainable for themselves. The second effect is that they regard the possessors of property as a class apart, whom they always must ultimately obey, often envy, and sometimes hate ; whose moral right to so singular a position most of them would hesitate to concede, and many of them would now strongly deny, but whose position they, at any rate, accept as a known and permanent social fact, the origins of which they have forgotten, and the foundations of which they believe to be immemorial.

To sum up: The attitude of the proletariat in England to-day (the attitude of the overwhelming majority, that is, of English families) towards property and towards that freedom which is alone obtainable through property is no longer an attitude of experience or of expectation. They think of themselves as wage-earners. To increase the weekly stipend of the wage-earner is an object which they vividly appreciate and pursue. To make him cease to be a wage-earner is an object that would seem to them entirely outside the realities of life.

What of the second factor, the gambling chance which the Capitalist system, with its necessary condition of freedom, of the legal power to bargain fully, and so forth, permits to the proletarian of escaping from his proletariat surroundings ?

Of this gambling chance and the effect it has upon men's minds we may say that, while it has not disappeared, it has very greatly lost in force during the last forty years. One often meets men who tell one, whether they are speaking in defence of or against the Capitalist system, that it still blinds the proletarian to any common consciousness of class, because the proletarian still has the example before him of members of his class, whom he has known, rising (usually by various forms of villainy) to the position of capitalist. But when one goes down among the working men themselves, one discovers that the hope of such a change in the mind of any individual worker is now exceedingly remote. Millions of men in great groups of industry, notably in the transport industry and in the mines, have quite given up such an expectation. Tiny as the chance ever was, exaggerated as the hopes in a lottery always are, that tiny chance has fallen in the general opinion of the workers to be negligible, and that hope which a lottery breeds is extinguished. The proletarian now regards himself as definitely proletarian, nor destined within human likelihood to be anything but proletarian.

These two factors, then, the memory of an older condition of economic freedom, and the effect of a hope individuals might entertain of escaping from the wage-earning class, the two factors which might act most strongly *against* the acceptation of the Servile State by that class, have so fallen in value that they offer but little opposition to the third factor in the situation which is making so strongly *for* the Servile State, and which consists in the necessity all men acutely feel for sufficiency and for security. It is this third factor alone which need be seriously considered to-day, when we ask ourselves how far the material upon which social reform is working, that is, the masses of the people, may be ready to accept the change.

The thing may be put in many ways. I will put it in what I believe to be the most conclusive of all.

If you were to approach those millions of families now living at a wage, with the proposal for a contract of service for life, guaranteeing them employment at what each regarded as his usual full wage, how many would refuse?

Such a contract would, of course, involve a loss of freedom: a life-contract of the kind is, to be accurate, no contract at all. It is the negation of contract and the acceptation of status. It would lay the man that undertook it under an obligation of forced labour, coterminous and coincident with his power to labour. It would be a permanent renunciation of his right (if such a right exists) to the surplus values created by his labour. If we ask ourselves how many men, or rather how many families, would prefer freedom (with its accompaniments of certain insecurity and possible insufficiency) to such a life-contract, no one can deny that the answer is : " Very few would refuse it." That is the key to the whole matter.

What proportion would refuse it no one can determine; but I say that even as a voluntary offer, and not as a compulsory obligation, a contract of this sort which would for the future destroy contract and re-erect status of a servile sort would be thought a boon by the mass of the proletariat to-day.

Now take the truth from another aspect—by considering it thus from one point of view and from another we can appreciate it best—Of what are the mass of men now most afraid in a Capitalist State ? Not of the punishments that can be inflicted by a Court of Law, but of " the sack."

You may ask a man why he does not resist such and such a legal infamy ; why he permits himself to be the victim of fines and deductions from which the Truck Acts specifically protect him ; why he cannot assert his opinion in this or that matter ; why he has accepted, without a blow, such and such an insult.

THE SERVILE STATE

Some generations ago a man challenged to tell you why he forswore his manhood in any particular regard would have answered you that it was because he feared punishment at the hands of the law; to-day he will tell you that it is because he fears unemployment.

Private law has for the second time in our long European story overcome public law, and the sanctions which the Capitalist can call to the aid of his private rule, by the action of his private will, are stronger than those which the public Courts can impose.

In the seventeenth century a man feared to go to Mass lest the judges should punish him. To-day a man fears to speak in favour of some social theory which he holds to be just and true lest his master should punish him. To deny the rule of public powers once involved public punishments which most men dreaded, though some stood out. To deny the rule of private powers involves to-day a private punishment against the threat of which very few indeed dare to stand out.

Look at the matter from yet another aspect. A law is passed (let us suppose) which increases the total revenue of a wage-earner, or guarantees him against the insecurity of his position in some small degree. The administration of that law requires, upon the one hand, a close inquisition into the man's circumstances by public officials, and, upon the other hand, the administration of its benefits by that particular Capitalist or group of Capitalists whom the wage-earner serves to enrich. Do the Servile conditions attaching to this material benefit prevent a proletarian in England to-day from preferring the benefit to freedom? It is notorious that they do not.

No matter from what angle you approach the business, the truth is always the same. That great mass of wage-earners upon which our society now reposes understands as a present good all that will increase even to some small amount their present revenue and all that may guarantee them against those perils of insecurity to which they are perpetually subject. They understand and welcome a good of this kind, and they are perfectly willing to pay for that good the corresponding price of control and enregimentation, exercised in gradually increasing degree by those who are their paymasters.

It would be easy by substituting superficial for fundamental things, or even by proposing certain terms and phrases to be used in the place of terms and phrases now current—it would be easy, I say, by such methods to ridicule or to oppose the prime truths which I am here submitting. They none the less remain truths.

Substitute for the term "employee" in one of our new laws the term "serf," even do so mild a thing as to substitute the traditional term "master" for the word "employer," and the blunt words might breed revolt. Impose of a sudden the full conditions of a Servile State upon modern England, and it would certainly breed revolt. But my point is that when the foundations of the thing have to be laid and the first great steps taken, there is no revolt; on the contrary, there is acquiescence and for the most part gratitude upon the part of the poor. After the long terrors imposed upon them through a freedom unaccompanied by property, they see, at the expense of losing a mere legal freedom, the very real prospect of *having enough* and *not losing it*.

All forces, then, are making for the Servile State in this the final phase of our evil Capitalist society in England. The generous reformer is canalised towards it ; the ungenerous one finds it a very mirror of his ideal; the herd of "practical" men meet at every stage in its inception the "practical" steps which they expected and demanded; while that proletarian mass upon whom the experiment is being tried have lost the tradition of property and of freedom which might resist the change, and are most powerfully inclined to its acceptance by the positive benefits which it confers.

It may be objected that however true all this may be, no one can, upon such theoretical grounds, regard the Servile State as something really approaching us. We need not believe in its advent (we shall be told) until we see the first effects of its action.

To this I answer that the first effects of its action are already apparent. The Servile State is, in industrial England to-day, no longer a menace but something in actual existence. It is in process of construction. The first main lines of it are already plotted out ; the corner-stone of it is already laid.

To see the truth of this I will next consider servile laws and projects of law, the first of which we already suffer, while the last will pass from project to positive statute in due process of time.

APPENDIX ON "BUYING-OUT"

There is an impression abroad among those who propose to expropriate the Capitalist class for the benefit of the State, but who appreciate the difficulties in the way of direct confiscation, that by spreading the process over a sufficient number of years and pursuing it after a certain fashion bearing all the outward appearances of a purchase, the expropriation could be effected without the consequences and attendant difficulties of direct confiscation. In other words, there is an impression that the State could "buy-out" the Capitalist class without their knowing it, and that in a sort of painless way this class can be slowly conjured out of existence.

The impression is held in a confused fashion by most of those who cherish it, and will not bear a clear analysis.

THE SERVILE STATE

It is impossible by any jugglery to "buy-out" the universality of the means of production without confiscation.

To prove this, consider a concrete case which puts the problem in the simplest terms:—

A community of twenty-two families lives upon the produce of two farms, the property of only two families out of that twenty-two.

The remaining twenty families are Proletarian. The two families, with their ploughs, stores, land, etc., are Capitalist.

The labour of the twenty proletarian families applied to the land and capital of these two capitalist families produces 300 measures of wheat, of which 200 measures, or 10 measures each, form the annual support of the twenty proletarian families ; the remaining 100 measures are the surplus value retained as rent, interest, and profit by the two Capitalist families, each of which has thus a yearly income of 50 measures.

The State proposes to produce, after a certain length of time, a condition of affairs such that the surplus values shall no longer go to the two Capitalist families, but shall be distributed to the advantage of the whole community, while it, the State, shall itself become the unembarrassed owner of both farms.

Now capital is accumulated with the object of a certain return as the reward of accumulation. Instead of spending his money, a man saves it with the object of retaining as the result of that saving a certain yearly revenue. The measure of this does not fall in a particular society at a particular time below a certain level. In other words, if a man cannot get a certain minimum reward for his accumulation, he will not accumulate but spend.

What is called in economics " The Law of Diminishing

Returns" acts so that continual additions to capital, other things being equal (that is, the methods of production remaining the same), do not provide a corresponding increase of revenue. A thousand measures of capital applied to a particular area of natural forces will produce, for instance, 40 measures yearly, or 4 per cent.; but 2000 measures applied in the same fashion will not produce 80 measures. They will produce more than the thousand measures did, but not more in proportion ; not double. They will produce, say, 60 measures, or 3 per cent., upon the capital. The action of this universal principle automatically checks the accumulation of capital when it has reached such a point that the proportionate return is the least which a man will accept. If it falls below that he will spend rather than accumulate. The limit of this minimum in any particular society at any particular time gives the measure to what we call "*the Effective Desire of Accumulation.*" Thus in England to-day it is a little over 3 per cent. The minimum which limits the accumulation of capital is a mimimum return of about one-thirtieth yearly upon such capital, and this we may call for shortness the " E.D.A." of our society at the present time.

When, therefore, the Capitalist estimates the full value of his possessions, he counts them in "so many years' purchase."* And that means that he is willing to take in a lump sum down for his possessions so many times the yearly revenue which he at present enjoys. If his E.D.A. is

* By an illusion which clever statesmanship could use to the advantage of the community, he even estimates the natural forces he controls (which need no accumulation, but are always present) on the analogy of his capital, and will part with them at " so many years' purchase." It is by taking advantage of this illusion that land purchase schemes (as in Ireland) happily work to the advantage of the dispossessed.

one-thirtieth, he will take a lump sum representing thirty times his annual revenue.

So far so good. Let us suppose the two Capitalists in our example to have an E.D.A. of one-thirtieth. They will sell to the State if the State can put up thirty times their surplus or "income," *i.e.* 3000 measures of wheat.

Now, of course, the State can do nothing of the kind. The accumulations of wheat being already in the hands of the Capitalists, and those accumulations amounting to much less than 3000 measures of wheat, the thing appears to be a deadlock.

But it is not a deadlock if the Capitalist is a fool. The State can go to the Capitalists and say : " Hand me over your farms, and against them I will give you guarantee that you shall be paid *rather more than* 100 measures of wheat a year for the thirty years. In fact, I will pay you half as much again until these extra payments amount to a purchase of your original stock."

Out of what does this extra amount come ? Out of the State's power to tax.

The State can levy a tax upon the profits of both Capitalists A and B, and pay them the extra with their own money.

In so simple an example it is evident that this "ringing of the changes" would be spotted by the victims, and that they would bring against it precisely the same forces which they would bring against the much simpler and more straightforward process of immediate confiscation.

But it is argued that in a complex State, where you are dealing with myriads of individual Capitalists and thousands of particular forms of profit, the process can be masked.

There are two ways in which the State can mask its

action (according to this policy). It can buy out first one small area of land and capital out of the general taxation and then another, and then another, until the whole has been transferred; or it can tax with peculiar severity certain trades which the rest who are left immune will abandon to their ruin, and with the general taxation plus this special taxation buy out those unfortunate trades which will, of course, have sunk heavily in value under the attack.

The second of these tricks will soon be apparent in any society, however complex; for after one unpopular trade had been selected for attack the trying on of the same methods in another less unpopular field will at once rouse suspicion.*

The first method, however, might have some chance of success, at least for a long time after it was begun, in a highly complex and numerous society were it not for a certain check which comes in of itself. That check is the fact that the Capitalist only takes *more than* his old yearly revenue with the object of reinvesting the surplus.

I have a thousand pounds in Brighton railway stock, yielding me 3 per cent. : £30 a year. The Government asks me to exchange my bit of paper against another bit of paper guaranteeing the payment of £50 a year, that is, an extra rate a year, for so many years as will represent over and above the regular interest paid a purchase of my stock. The Government's bit of paper promises to pay to the holder £50 a year for, say, thirty-eight years. I am delighted to make the exchange, not because I am such a fool as to enjoy the prospect of my property being extinguished at the end of thirty-eight years, but because I hope

---

* Thus you can raid the brewers in a society half-Puritan where brewing is thought immoral by many, but proceed to railway stock and it will be a very different matter.

to be able to reinvest the extra £20 every year in something else that will bring me in £ per cent. Thus, at the end of the thirty-eight years I shall (or my heirs) be better off than I was at the beginning of the transaction, and I shall have enjoyed during its maturing my old £30 a year all the same.

The State can purchase thus on a small scale by subsidising purchase out of the general taxation. It can, therefore, play this trick over a small area and for a short time with success. But the moment this area passes a very narrow limit the " market for investment " is found to be restricted, Capital automatically takes alarm, the State can no longer offer its paper guarantees save at an enhanced price. If it tries to turn the position by further raising taxation to what Capital regards as " confiscatory " rates, there will be opposed to its action just the same forces as would be opposed to frank and open expropriation.

The matter is one of plain arithmetic, and all the confusion introduced by the complex mechanism of "finance" can no more change the fundamental and arithmetical principles involved than can the accumulation of triangles in an ordnance survey reduce the internal angles of the largest triangle to less than 180 degrees.* In fine : *if you desire to confiscate, you must confiscate.*

You cannot outflank the enemy, as Financiers in the city and sharpers on the race-course outflank the simpler of mankind, nor can you conduct the general process of expropriation upon a muddle-headed hope that somehow or other something will come out of nothing in the end.

There are, indeed, two ways in which the State could ex-

* In using this metaphor I at once record my apologies to those who believe in elliptical and hyperbolic universes, and confess myself an old-fashioned parabolist. Further, I admit that the triangles in question are spherical.

propriate without meeting the resistance that must be present against any attempt at confiscation. But the first of these ways is precarious, the second insufficient.

They are as follows:—

(1) The State can promise the Capitalist a larger yearly revenue than he is getting in the expectation that it, the State, can manage the business better than the Capitalist, or that some future expansion will come to its aid. In other words, if the State makes a bigger profit out of the thing than the Capitalist, it can buy out the Capitalist just as a private individual with a similar business proposition can buy him out.

But the converse of this is that if the State has calculated badly, or has bad luck, it would find itself *endowing* the Capitalists of the future instead of gradually extinguishing them.

In this fashion the State could have "socialised" without confiscation the railways of this country if it had taken them over fifty years ago, promising the then owners more than they were then obtaining. But if it had socialised the hansom cab in the nineties, it would now be supporting in perpetuity that worthy but extinct type the cab-owner (and his children for ever) at the expense of the community.

The second way in which the State can expropriate without confiscation is by annuity. It can say to such Capitalists as have no heirs or care little for their fate if they have : " You have only got so much time to live and to enjoy your £30, will you take £50 until you die ? " Upon the bargain being accepted the State will, in process of time, though not immediately upon the death of the annuitant, become an unembarrassed owner of what had been the annuitant's share in the means of production. But the area over which this method can be exercised is a very small one. It is not of itself a sufficient instrument for the expropriation of any considerable field.

I need hardly add that as a matter of fact the so-called "Socialist" and confiscatory measures of our time have nothing to do with the problem here discussed. The State is indeed confiscating, that is, it is taxing in many cases in such a fashion as to impoverish the tax-payer and is lessening his capital rather than shearing his income. But it is not putting the proceeds into the means of production. It is either using them for immediate consumption in the shape of new official salaries or handing them over to another set of Capitalists.*

But these practical considerations of the way in which sham Socialist experiments are working belong rather to my next section, in which I shall deal with the actual beginnings of the Servile State in our midst.

* Thus the money levied upon the death of some not very wealthy squire and represented by, say, locomotives in the Argentine, turns into two miles of palings for the pleasant back gardens of a thousand new officials under the Inebriates Bill, or is simply handed over to the shareholders of the Prudential under the Insurance Act. In the first case the locomotives have been given back to the Argentine, and after a long series of exchanges have been bartered against a great number of wood-palings from the Baltic—not exactly reproductive wealth. In the second case the locomotives which used to be the squire's hands become, or their equivalent becomes, means of production in the hands of the Sassoons.

SECTION NINE

THE SERVILE STATE
HAS BEGUN

IN THIS LAST DIVISION OF MY BOOK I
deal with the actual appearance of the Servile State
in certain laws and proposals now familiar to the
Industrial Society of modern England. These are
the patent objects, "laws and projects of laws," which
lend stuff to my argument, and show that it is based
not upon a mere deduction, but upon an observation
of things.

Two forms of this proof are evident: first, the laws
and proposals which subject the *Proletariat* to Servile
conditions ; next, the fact that the *Capitalist*, so far
from being expropriated by modern " Socialist " experiments, is being confirmed in his power.

I take these in their order, and I begin by asking
in what statutes or proposals the Servile State first
appeared among us.

A false conception of our subject might lead one
to find the origins of the Servile State in the restrictions imposed upon certain forms of manufacture,
and the corresponding duties laid upon the Capitalist in the interest of his workmen. The Factory Laws,
as they are in this country, would seem to offer upon
this superficial and erroneous view a starting point.
They do nothing of the kind ; and the view *is* superficial and erroneous because it neglects the funda-
mentals of the case. What distinguishes the Servile
State is not the interference of law with the action

of any citizen even in connection with industrial matters. Such interference may or may not indicate the presence of a Servile status. It in no way indicates the presence of that status when it forbids a particular kind of human action to be undertaken by the citizen as a citizen.

The legislator says, for instance, "You may pluck roses; but as I notice that you sometimes scratch yourself, I will put you in prison unless you cut them with scissors at least 122 millimetres long, and I will appoint one thousand inspectors to go round the country seeing whether the law is observed. My brother-in-law shall be at the head of the Department at £2000 a year."

We are all familiar with that type of legislation. We are all familiar with the arguments for and against it in any particular case. We may regard it as onerous, futile, or beneficent, or in any other light, according to our various temperaments. But it does not fall within the category of servile legislation, because it establishes no distinction between two classes of citizens, marking off the one as legally distinct from the other by a criterion of manual labour or of income.

This is even true of such regulations as those which compel a Cotton Mill, for instance, to have no less than such and such an amount of cubic space for each operative, and such and such protection for dangerous machinery. These laws do not concern themselves with the nature, the amount, or even the existence of a contract for service. The object, for example, of the law which compels one to fence off certain types of machinery is simply to protect human life, regardless of whether the human being so protected is rich or poor, Capitalist or Proletarian. These laws may in effect work in our society so that the Capitalist is made responsible for the Proletarian, but he is not responsible *quâ* Capitalist, nor is the Proletarian protected *quâ* Proletarian.

In the same way the law may compel me, if I am a Riparian owner, to put up a fence of statutory strength wherever the water of my river is of more than a statutory depth. Now it cannot compel me to do this unless I am the owner of the land. In a sense, therefore, this might be called the recognition of my *Status*, because, by the nature of the case, only landowners can be affected by the law, and landowners would be compelled by it to safeguard the lives of all, whether they were or were not owners of land.

But the category so established would be purely accidental. The object and method of the law do not concern themselves with a distinction between citizens.

A close observer might indeed discover certain points in the Factory laws, details and phrases, which did distinctly connote the existence of a Capitalist and of a Proletarian class. But we must take the statutes as a whole and the order in which they were produced, above all, the general motive and expressions governing each main statute, in order to judge whether such examples of interference give us an origin or not.

The verdict will be that they do not. Such legislation may be oppressive in any degree or necessary in any degree, but it does not establish status in the place of contract, and it is not, therefore, servile.

Neither are those laws servile which in practice attach to the poor and not to the rich. Compulsory education is in legal theory required of every citizen for his children. The state of mind which goes with plutocracy exempts of course all above a certain standard of wealth from this law. But the law does apply to the universality of the commonwealth, and all families resident in Great Britain (not in Ireland) are subject to its provisions.

These are not origins. A true origin to servile and " statu s" legislation comes later. The first example of servile legislation to be discovered upon the Statute Book is that which establishes the present form of *Employer's Liability*.

I am far from saying that that law was passed, as modern laws are beginning to be passed, with the direct object of establishing a new status; though it was passed with some consciousness on the part of the

158

legislator that such a new status was in existence as a social fact. Its motive was merely humane, and the relief which it afforded seemed merely necessary at the time; but it is an instructive example of the way in which a small neglect of strict doctrine and a slight toleration of anomaly admit great changes into the State.

There had existed from all time in every community, and there was founded upon common sense, the legal doctrine that if one citizen was so placed with regard to another by contract that he must in the fulfilment of that contract perform certain services, and if those services accidentally involved damages to a third party, not the actual perpetrator of the damage, but he who designed the particular operation leading to it was responsible.

The point is subtle, but, as I say, fundamental. It involved no distinction of status between employer and employed.

Citizen A offered citizen B a sack of wheat down if citizen B would plough for him a piece of land which might or might not produce more than a sack of wheat.

Of course citizen A expected it would produce more, and was awaiting a surplus value, or he would not have made the contract with citizen B. But, at any rate, citizen B put his name to the agreement, and as a free man, capable of contracting, was correspondingly bound to fulfil it.

In fulfilling this contract the ploughshare B is driving destroys a pipe conveying water by agreement through A's land to C. C suffers damage, and to recover the equivalent of that damage his action in justice and common sense can only be against A, for B was carrying out a plan and instruction of which A was the author. C is a third party who had nothing to do with such a contract and could not possibly have justice save by his chances of getting it from A, who was the true author of the unintentional loss inflicted, since he designed the course of work.

But when the damage is not done to C at all, but to B, who is concerned with a work the risks of which are known and willingly undertaken, it is quite another matter.

Citizen A contracts with citizen B that citizen B, in consideration of a sack of wheat, shall plough a bit of land. Certain known risks must attach to that operation. Citizen B, if he is a free man, undertakes those risks with his eyes open. For instance, he may sprain his wrist in turning the plough, or one of the horses may kick him while he is having his bread-and-cheese. If upon such an accident A is compelled to pay damages to B, a difference of status is at once recognised. B undertook to do work which, by all the theory of free contract, was, with its risks and its expense of energy, the equivalent in B's own eyes of a sack of wheat; yet a law is passed to say that B can have more than that sack of wheat if he is hurt.

There is no converse right of A against B. If the employer suffers by such an accident to the employee, *he* is not allowed to dock that sack of wheat, though it was regarded in the contract as the equivalent to a certain amount of labour to be performed which, as a fact, has not been performed. A has no action unless B has been *culpably* negligent or remiss. In other words, the mere fact that one man is *working* and the other not is the fundamental consideration on which the law is built, and the law says: "You are not a free man making a free contract with all its consequences. You are a worker, and therefore an inferior: you are an *employee*; and that *status* gives you a special position which would not be recognised in the other party to the contract."

The principle is pushed still further when an employer is made liable for an accident happening to one of his employees at the hands of another employee.

A gives a sack of wheat to B and D each if they will dig a well for him. All three parties are cognisant of the risks and accept them in the contract. B, holding the rope on which D is lowered, lets it slip. If they were all three men of exactly equal status, obviously D's action would be against B. But they are not of equal status in England to-day. B and D are *mployees*, and are therefore in a special and inferior position before the law compared with their employer A. D's action is, by this novel principle, no longer against B, who accidentally injured him by a personal act, however involuntary, for which a free man would be responsible, but against A, who was innocent of the whole business.

Now in all this it is quite clear that A has peculiar duties not because he is a citizen, but because he is something more: *an employer;* and B and D have special claims on A, not because they are citizens, but because they are something less: *viz. employees.* They can *claim protection* from A, as inferiors of a superior in a State admitting such distinctions and patronage.

It will occur at once to the reader that in our existing social state the employee will be very grateful for such legislation. One workman cannot recover from another—simply because the other will have no goods out of which to pay damages. Let the burden, therefore, fall upon the rich man!

Excellent. But that is not the point. To argue thus is to say that Servile legislation is necessary if we are to solve the problems raised by Capitalism. It remains servile legislation none the less. It is legislation that would not exist in a society where property was well divided and where a citizen could normally pay damages for the harm he had himself caused.*

* How true it is that the idea of status underlies this legislation can easily be tested by taking parallel cases, in one of which

SERVILE STATE HAS BEGUN

This first trickle of the stream, however, though it is of considerable historical interest as a point of departure, is not of very definite moment to our subject compared with the great bulk of later proposals, some of which are already law, others upon the point of becoming law, and which definitely recognise the Servile State, the re-establishment of status in the place of contract, and the universal division of citizens into two categories of employers and employed.

These last merit a very different consideration, for they will represent to history the conscious and designed entry of Servile Institutions into the old Christian State. They are not "origins," small indications of coming change which the historian will painfully discover as a curiosity. They are the admitted foundations of a new order, deliberately planned by a few, confusedly accepted by the many, as the basis upon which a novel and stable society shall arise to replace the unstable and passing phase of Capitalism.

working men are concerned, in the other the professional class. If I contract to write for a publisher a complete History of the County of Rutland, and in the pursuit of that task, while examining some object of historical interest, fall down a pit, I should not be able to recover against the publisher. But if I dress in mean clothes, and the same publisher, deceived, gives me a month's work at cleaning out his ornamental water and I am wounded in that occupation by a fierce fish, he will be mulcted to my advantage, and that roundly.

They fall roughly into three categories :—

(1) Measures by which the insecurity of the proletariat shall be relieved through the action of the employing class, or of the proletariat itself acting under compulsion.

(2) Measures by which the employer shall be compelled to give not less than a certain minimum for any labour he may purchase, and

(3) Measures which compel a man lacking the means of production to labour, though he may have made no contract to that effect.

The last two, as will be seen in a moment, are complementary one of another.

As to the first: Measures to palliate the insecurity of the proletariat.

We have of this an example in actual law at this moment. And that law—the Insurance Act—(whose political source and motive I am not here discussing) follows in every particular the lines of a Servile State.

(*a*) Its fundamental criterion is employment. In other words, I am compelled to enter a scheme providing me against the mischances of illness and unemployment not because I am a citizen, but only if I am:

(1) Exchanging services for goods ; and either

(2) Obtaining less than a certain amount of goods for those services, or

(3) A vulgar fellow working with his hands.

The law carefully excludes from its provisions those

orms of labour to which the educated and therefore powerful classes are subject, and further excludes from compulsion the mass of those who are for the moment earning enough to make them a class to be reckoned with as economically free. I may be a writer of books who, should he fall ill, will leave in the greatest distress the family which he supports. If the legislator were concerned for the morals of citizens, I should most undoubtedly come under this law, under the form of compulsory insurance added to my income tax. But the legislator is not concerned with people of my sort. He is concerned with a new status which he recognises in the State, to wit, the proletariat. He envisages the proletariat not quite accurately as men either poor, or, they are not poor, at any rate vulgar people working with their hands, and he legislates accordingly.

(b) Still more striking, as an example of status taking the place of contract, is the fact that this law puts the duty of controlling the proletariat and of seeing that the law is obeyed *not* upon the proletariat itself, but upon the *Capitalist class.*

Now this point is of an importance that cannot be exaggerated.

The future historian, whatever his interest in the first indications of that profound revolution through which we are so rapidly passing, will most certainly fix upon that one point as the cardinal landmark of our times. The legislator surveying the Capitalist

State proposes as a remedy for certain of its evils the establishment of two categories in the State, compel the lower man to registration, to a tax, and the rest o it, and further compels the upper man to be the instru ment in enforcing that registration and in collecting that tax. No one acquainted with the way in which any one of the great changes of the past has taken place the substitution of tenure for the Roman proprietary right in land, or the substitution of the mediæval peas ant for the serf of the Dark Ages, can possibly mis understand the significance of such a turning poin in our history.

Whether it will be completed or whether a reactio will destroy it is another matter. Its mere propose is of the greatest possible moment in the inquiry w are here pursuing.

Of the next two groups, the fixing of a Minimu Wage and the Compulsion to Labour (which, as I hav said, and will shortly show, are complementary on to the other), neither has yet appeared in actual legis lation, but both are planned, both thought out, bot possessed of powerful advocates, and both upon th threshold of positive law.

The fixing of a Minimum Wage, with a definit sum fixed by statute, has not yet* entered our law but the first step towards such a consummation ha

* September 1912.

been taken in the shape of giving legal sanction to some hypothetical Minimum Wage which shall be arrived at after discussion within a particular trade. That trade is, of course, the mining industry. The law does not say: "No Capitalist shall pay a miner less than so many shillings for so many hours' work." But it does say: "Figures having been arrived at by local boards, any miner working within the area of each board can claim by force of law the minimum sum established by such boards." It is evident that from this step to the next, which shall define some sliding scale of remuneration for labour according to prices and the profits of capital, is an easy and natural transition. It would give both parties what each immediately requires: to capital a guarantee against disturbance; to labour sufficiency and security. The whole thing is an excellent object lesson in little of that general movement from free contract to status, and from the Capitalist to the Servile State, which is the tide of our time.

The neglect of older principles as abstract and doctrinaire; the immediate need of both parties immediately satisfied; the unforeseen but necessary consequence of satisfying such needs in such a fashion—all these, which are apparent in the settlement the mining industry has begun, are the typical forces producing the Servile State.

Consider in its largest aspect the nature of such a settlement.

THE SERVILE STATE

The Proletarian accepts a position in which he pro
duces for the Capitalist a certain total of economi
values, and retains out of that total a portion only
leaving to the Capitalist all surplus value. The Capi
talist, on his side, is guaranteed in the secure an
permanent expectation of that surplus value throug
all the perils of social envy; the Proletarian is guar
anteed in a sufficiency and a security for that suffi
ciency ; but by the very action of such a guarante
there is withdrawn from him the power to refuse hi
labour and thus to aim at putting himself in posses
sion of the means of production.

Such schemes definitely divide citizens into tw
classes, the Capitalist and the Proletarian. They mak
it impossible for the second to combat the privilege
position of the first. They introduce into the positiv
laws of the community a recognition of social fact
which already divide Englishmen into two groups
economically more free and economically less fre
and they stamp with the authority of the State
new constitution of society. Society is recognised a
no longer consisting of free men bargaining freely fo
their labour or any other commodity in their posses
sion, but of two contrasting status, owners and no
owners. The first must not be allowed to leave th
second without subsistence ; the second must not b
allowed to obtain that grip upon the means of pr
duction which is the privilege of the first. It is tr

that this first experiment is small in degree and tentative in quality; but to judge the movement as a general whole we must not only consider the expression it has actually received so far in positive law, but the mood of our time.

When this first experiment in a minimum wage was being debated in Parliament, what was the great issue of debate? Upon what did those who were the most ardent reformers particularly insist? *Not* that the miners should have an avenue open to them for obtaining possession of the mines; not even that the State should have an avenue open to it for obtaining such possession; *but that the minimum wage should be fixed at a certain satisfactory level*! That, as our recent experience testifies for all of us, was the crux of the quarrel. And that such a point should be the crux, not the socialisation of the mines, nor the admission of the proletariat to the means of production, but only a sufficiency and a security of wage, is amply significant of the perhaps irresistible forces which are making in the direction for which I argue in this book.

There was here no attempt of the Capitalist to impose Servile conditions nor of the Proletarian to resist them. Both parties were agreed upon that fundamental change. The discussion turned upon the minimum limit of subsistence to be securely provided, a point which left aside, because it took for granted, the establishment of *some* minimum in any case.

169

Next, let it be noted (for it is of moment to a later part of my argument) that experiments of this sort promise to extend piecemeal. There is no likelihood, judging by men's actions and speech, of some grand general scheme for the establishment of a minimum wage throughout the community. Such a scheme would, of course, be as truly an establishment of the Servile State as piecemeal schemes. But, as we shall see in a moment, the extension of the principle piecemeal has a considerable effect upon the forms which compulsion may take.

The miners' refusal to work, with the exaggerated panic it caused, bred this first tentative appearance of the minimum wage in our laws. Normally, capital prefers free labour with its margin of destitution; for such an anarchy, ephemeral though it is of its nature, while it lasts provides cheap labour; from the narrowest point of view it provides in the still competitive areas of Capitalism a better chance for profits.

But as one group of workmen after another, concerned with trades immediately necessary to the life of the nation, and therefore tolerating but little interruption, learn the power which combination gives them, it is inevitable that the legislator (concentrated as he is upon momentary remedies for difficulties as they arise) should propose for one such trade after another the remedy of a minimum wage.

There can be little doubt that, trade by trade, the

principle will extend. For instance, the two and a half millions now guaranteed against unemployment are guaranteed against it for a certain weekly sum. That weekly sum must bear some relation to their estimated earnings when they are in employment.

It is a short step from the calculation of unemployment benefit (its being fixed by statute at a certain level, and that level determined by something which is regarded as the just remuneration of labour in that trade); it is a short step, I say, from that to a statutory fixing of the sums paid during employment.

The State says to the Serf: "I saw to it that you should have so much when you were unemployed. I find that in some rare cases my arrangement leads to your getting more when you are unemployed than when you are employed. I further find that in many cases, though you get more when you are employed, yet the difference is not sufficient to tempt a lazy man to work, or to make him take any particular trouble to get work. I must see to this."

The provision of a fixed schedule during unemployment thus inevitably leads to the examination, the defining, and at last the imposition of a minimum wage during employment; and every compulsory provision for unemployed benefits is the seed of a minimum wage.

Of still greater effect is the mere presence of State regulation in such a matter. The fact that the State has begun to gather statistics of wages over these large areas of industry, and to do so not for a mere statistical object, but a practical one, and the fact that the State has begun to immix the action of positive law and constraint with the older system of free bargaining, mean that the whole weight of its influence is now in favour of regulation. It is no rash prophecy to assert that in the near future our industrial society will see a gradually extending area of industry in which from two sides the fixing of wages by statute shall appear. From the one side it will come in the form of the State examining the conditions of labour in connection with its own schemes for establishing sufficiency and security by insurance. From the other side it will come through the reasonable proposals to make contracts enforceable in the Courts between groups of labour and groups of capital.

So much, then, for the Principle of a Minimum Wage. It has already appeared in our laws. It is certain to spread. But how does the presence of this introduction of a Minimum form part of the advance towards the Servile State?

I have said that the principle of a minimum wage involves as its converse the principle of compulsory labour. Indeed, most of the importance which the principle of a minimum wage has for this inquiry lies in that converse necessity of compulsory labour which it involves.

But as the connection between the two may not be clear at first sight, we must do more than take it for granted. We must establish it by process of reason.

There are two distinct forms in which the whole policy of enforcing security and sufficiency by law for the proletariat produce a corresponding policy of compulsory labour.

The first of these forms is the compulsion which the Courts will exercise upon either of the parties concerned in the giving and in the receiving of the minimum wage. The second form is the necessity under which society will find itself, when once the principle of the minimum wage is conceded, coupled with the principle of sufficiency and security, to control those whom the minimum wage excludes from the area of normal employment.

As to the first form :—

A Proletarian group has struck a bargain with a group of Capitalists to the effect that it will produce for that capital ten measures of value in a year, will be content to receive six measures of value for itself, and will leave four measures as surplus value for the Capitalists. The bargain is ratified ; the Courts have the power to enforce it. If the Capitalists by some trick of fines or by bluntly breaking their word pay out in wages less than the six measures, the Courts must

have some power of constraining them. In other
words, there must be some sanction to the action of
the law. There must be some power of punishment,
and, through punishment, of compulsion. Conversely
if the men, having struck this bargain, go back upon
their word ; if individuals among them or sections
among them cease work with a new demand for seven
measures instead of six, the Courts must have the
power of constraining and of punishing *them*. Where
the bargain is ephemeral or at any rate extended over
only reasonable limits of time, it would be straining
language perhaps to say that each individual case of
constraint exercised against the workmen would be
a case of compulsory labour. But extend the system
over a long period of years, make it normal to industry and accepted as a habit in men's daily conception of the way in which their lives should be conducted, and the method is necessarily transformed
into a system of compulsory labour. In trades where
wages fluctuate little this will obviously be the case.
" You, the agricultural labourers of this district, have
taken fifteen shillings a week for a very long time.
It has worked perfectly well. There seems no reason
why you should have more. Nay, you put your hands
to it through your officials in the year so and so that
you regarded that sum as sufficient. Such and such
of your members are now refusing to perform what
this Court regards as a contract. They must return

17

within the limits of that contract or suffer the consequences."

Remember what power analogy exercises over men's minds, and how, when systems of the sort are common to many trades, they will tend to create a general point of view for all trades. Remember also how comparatively slight a threat is already sufficient to control men in our industrial society, the proletarian mass of which is accustomed to live from week to week under peril of discharge, and has grown readily amenable to the threat of any reduction in those wages upon which it can but just subsist.

Nor are the Courts enforcing such contracts or quasi-contracts (as they will come to be regarded) the only inducement.

A man has been compelled by law to put aside sums from his wages as insurance against unemployment. But he is no longer the judge of how such sums shall be used. They are not in his possession ; they are not even in the hands of some society which he can really control. They are in the hands of a Government official. " Here is work offered you at twenty-five shillings a week. If you do not take it you certainly shall not have a right to the money you have been compelled to put aside. If you will take it the sum shall still stand to your credit, and when next in my judgment your unemployment is not due to your recalcitrance and refusal to labour,

THE SERVILE STATE

I will permit you to have some of your money: not otherwise." Dovetailing in with this machinery of compulsion is all that mass of registration and docketing which is accumulating through the use of Labour Exchanges. Not only will the Official have the power to enforce special contracts, or the power to coerce individual men to labour under the threat of a fine, but he will also have a series of *dossiers* by which the record of each workman can be established. No man, once so registered and known, can escape; and, of the nature of the system, the numbers caught in the net must steadily increase until the whole mass of labour is mapped out and controlled.

These are very powerful instruments of compulsion indeed. They already exist. They are already a part of our laws.

Lastly, there is the obvious bludgeon of "compulsory arbitration": a bludgeon so obvious that it is revolting even to our proletariat. Indeed, I know of no civilised European state which has succumbed to so gross a suggestion. For it is a frank admission of servitude at one step, and for good and all, such as men of our culture are not yet prepared to swallow.*

So much, then, for the first argument and the first form in which compulsory labour is seen to be a direct and necessary consequence of establishing a mi-

---

* But it has twice been brought forward in due process as a Bill in Parliament!

nimum wage and of scheduling employment to a scale.

The second is equally clear. In the production of wheat the healthy and skilled man who can produce ten measures of wheat is compelled to work for six measures, and the Capitalist is compelled to remain content with four measures for his share. The law will punish him if he tries to get out of his legal obligation and to pay his workmen less than six measures of wheat during the year. What of the man who is not sufficiently strong or skilled to produce even six measures ? Will the Capitalist be constrained to pay him more than the values he can produce ? Most certainly not. The whole structure of production as it was erected during the Capitalist phase of our industry has been left intact by the new laws and customs. Profit is still left a necessity. If it were destroyed, still more if a loss were imposed by law, that would be a contradiction of the whole spirit in which all these reforms are being undertaken. They are being undertaken with the object of establishing stability where there is now instability, and of "reconciling," as the ironic phrase goes, "the interests of capital and labour." It would be impossible, without a general ruin, to compel capital to lose upon the man who is not worth even the minimum wage. How shall that element of insecurity and instability be eliminated? To support the man gratuitously because he cannot earn a minimum wage, when all the rest of the commonwealth is working for its guaranteed wages, is to put a premium upon incapacity and sloth. The man must be made to work. He must be taught, if possible, to produce those economic values, which are regarded as the minimum of sufficiency. He must be kept at that work even if he cannot produce the minimum, lest his presence as a free labourer should imperil the whole scheme of the minimum wage, and introduce at the same time a continuous element of instability. Hence he is necessarily a subject for forced labour. We have not yet in this country, established by force of law, the right to this form of compulsion, but it is an inevitable consequence of those other reforms which have just been reviewed. The "Labour Colony" (a prison so called because euphemism is necessary to every transition) will be erected to absorb this surplus, and that last form of compulsion will crown the edifice of these reforms. They will then be complete so far as the subject classes are concerned, and even though this particular institution of the "Labour Colony" (logically the last of all) precede in time other forms of compulsion, it will make the advent of those other forms of compulsion more certain, facile, and rapid.

There remains one last remark to be made upon

the concrete side of my subject. I have in this last section illustrated the tendency towards the Servile State from actual laws and actual projects with which all are to-day familiar in English industrial society, and I have shown how these are certainly establishing the proletariat in a novel, but to them satisfactory, Servile Status.

It remains to point out in a very few lines the complementary truth that what should be the very essence of Collectivist Reform, to wit, the translation of the means of production from the hands of private owners to the hands of public officials, is nowhere being attempted. So far from its being attempted, all so-called " Socialistic " experiments in municipalisation and nationalisation are merely increasing the dependence of the community upon the Capitalist class. To prove this, we need only observe that every single one of these experiments is effected by a loan.

Now what is meant in economic reality by these municipal loans and national loans raised for the purpose of purchasing certain small sections of the means of production ?

Certain Capitalists own a number of rails, cars, etc. They put to work upon these certain Proletarians, and the result is a certain total of economic values Let the surplus values obtainable by the Capitalists after the subsistence of the proletarians is provided for amount to £10,000 a year. We all know how a system of this sort is "Municipalised. A "loan" is raised. It bears "interest." It is saddled with a "sinking fund."

Now this loan is not really made in money, though the terms of it are in money. It is, at the end of a long string of exchanges, nothing more nor less than the loan of the cars, the rails, etc., by the Capitalists to the Municipality. And the Capitalists require, before they will strike the bargain, a guarantee that the whole of their old profit shall be paid to them, together with a further yearly sum, which after a certain number of years shall represent the original value of the concern when they handed it over. These last additional sums are called the " sinking fund "; the continued payment of the old surplus values is called the " interest."

In theory certain small sections of the means of production might be acquired in this way. That particular section would have been " socialised." The " Sinking Fund " (that is, the paying of the Capitalists for their plant by instalments) might be met out of the general taxation imposed on the community, considering how large that is compared with any one experiment of the kind. The "interest" may by good management be met out of the true profits of the tramways. At the end of a certain number of years the community will be in possession of the tramways, will no longer be exploited in this particular by Capitalism, will have bought out Capitalism from the

general taxes, and, in so far as the purchase money
paid has been consumed and not saved or invested
by the Capitalists, a small measure of "socialisation"
will have been achieved.

As a fact things are never so favourable.

In practice three conditions militate against even
these tiny experiments in expropriation: the fact that
the implements are always sold at much more than
their true value ; the fact that the purchase includes
non-productive things; and the fact that the rate of
borrowing is much faster than the rate of repayment.
These three adverse conditions lead in practice to
nothing but the riveting of Capitalism more securely
round the body of the State.

For what is it that is paid for when a tramway,
for instance, is taken over? Is it the true capital
alone, the actual plant, which is paid for, even at an
exaggerated price? Far from it! Over and above
the rails and the cars, there are all the commissions
that have been made, all the champagne luncheons,
all the lawyers' fees, all the compensations to this
man and to that man, all the bribes. Nor does this
exhaust the argument. Tramways represent a productive investment. What about pleasure gardens,
wash-houses, baths, libraries, monuments, and the
rest? The greater part of these things are the product of "loans." When you put up a public institution you borrow the bricks and the mortar and the

181

iron and the wood and the tiles from Capitalists, *and you pledge yourself to pay interest, and to produce a sinking fund precisely as though a town hall or a bath were a piece of reproductive machinery.*

To this must be added the fact that a considerable proportion of the purchases are failures : purchases of things just before they are driven out by some new invention ; while on the top of the whole business you have the fact that the borrowing goes on at a far greater rate than the repayment.

In a word, all these experiments up and down Europe during our generation, municipal and national, have resulted in an indebtedness to capital increasing rather more than twice, but not three times, as fast as the rate of repayment. The interest which capital demands with a complete indifference as to whether the loan is productive or non-productive amounts to rather more than $1\frac{1}{2}$ per cent. *excess* over the produce of the various experiments, even though we count in the most lucrative and successful of these, such as the state railways of many countries, and the thoroughly successful municipal enterprises of many modern towns.

Capitalism has seen to it that it shall be a winner and not a loser by this form of sham Socialism, as by every other. And the same forces which in practice forbid confiscation see to it that the attempt to mask confiscation by purchase shall not only fail, but shall turn against those who have not had the courage to make a frontal attack upon privilege.

With these concrete examples showing how Collectivism, in attempting its practice, does but confirm the Capitalist position, and showing how our laws have already begun to impose a Servile Status upon the Proletariat, I end the argumentative thesis of this book.

I believe I have proved my case.

The future of industrial society, and in particular of English society, left to its own direction, is a future in which subsistence and security shall be guaranteed for the Proletariat, but shall be guaranteed at the expense of the old political freedom and by the establishment of that Proletariat in a status really, though not nominally, servile. At the same time, the Owners will be guaranteed in their profits, the whole machinery of production in the smoothness of its working, and that stability which has been lost under the Capitalist phase of society will be found once more.

The internal strains which have threatened society during its Capitalist phase will be relaxed and eliminated, and the community will settle down upon that Servile basis which was its foundation before the advent of the Christian faith, from which that faith slowly weaned it, and to which in the decay of that faith it naturally returns.

183

CONCLUSION

CONCLUSION

IT IS POSSIBLE TO PORTRAY A GREAT
social movement of the past with accuracy and in
detail if one can spare to the task the time necessary
for research and further bring to it a certain power of
co-ordination by which a great mass of detail can be
integrated and made one whole.

Such a task is rarely accomplished, but it does not
exceed the powers of history.

With regard to the future it is otherwise. No one
can say even in its largest aspect or upon its chief
structural line what that future will be. He can only
present the main tendencies of his time: he can only
determine the equation of the curve and presume that
that equation will apply more or less to its next developments.

So far as I can judge, those societies which broke
with the continuity of Christian civilisation in the sixteenth century—which means, roughly, North Germany and Great Britain—tend at present to the re-
establishment of a Servile Status. It will be diversi-
fied by local accident, modified by local character,
hidden under many forms. But it will come.

That the mere Capitalist anarchy cannot endure
is patent to all men. That only a very few possible
solutions to it exist should be equally patent to all.
For my part, as I have said in these pages, I do not
believe there are more than two: a reaction towards
well-divided property, or the re-establishment of ser-
187

vitude. I cannot believe that theoretical Collectivism, now so plainly failing, will ever inform a real and living society.

But my conviction that the re-establishment of the Servile Status in industrial society is actually upon us does not lead me to any meagre and mechanical prophecy of what the future of Europe shall be. The force of which I have been speaking is not the only force in the field. There is a complex knot of forces underlying any nation once Christian; a smouldering of the old fires.

Moreover, one can point to European societies which will most certainly reject any such solution of our Capitalist problem, just as the same societies have either rejected, or lived suspicious of, Capitalism itself, and have rejected or lived suspicious of that industrial organisation which till lately identified itself with "progress" and national well-being.

These societies are in the main the same as those which, in that great storm of the sixteenth century, —the capital episode in the story of Christendom— held fast to tradition and saved the continuity of morals. Chief among them should be noted to-day the French and the Irish.

I would record it as an impression (and no more) that the Servile State, strong as the tide is making for it in Prussia and in England to-day, will be modified, checked, perhaps defeated in war, certainly halted

188

CONCLUSION

in its attempt to establish itself completely, by the strong reaction which these freer societies upon its flank will perpetually exercise.

Ireland has decided for a free peasantry, and our generation has seen the solid foundation of that institution laid. In France the many experiments which elsewhere have successfully introduced the Servile State have been contemptuously rejected by the populace, and (most significant!) a recent attempt to register and to "insure" the artisans as a separate category of citizens has broken down in the face of an universal and a virile contempt.

That this second factor in the development of the future, the presence of free societies, will destroy the tendency to the Servile State elsewhere I do not affirm, but I believe that it will modify that tendency, certainly by example and perhaps by direct attack. And as I am upon the whole hopeful that the Faith will recover its intimate and guiding place in the heart of Europe, so I believe that this sinking back into our original Paganism (for the tendency to the Servile State is nothing less) will in due time be halted and reversed.

Videat Deus.